Other books by the author...

Pearls: Scriptures To Live By
    Mental health Bible concordance. Over 2,500 Scriptures for counsel and guidance. Compiled under 172 mental health topics.

Christlike: Walking The Walk
    A Scripture-based description of what it means to be a mentally healthy Christian, and how to become more Christlike.

Visit the author at...

Counseling4Christians.com

The #1 Christian Counseling
Internet Site on the Web

To schedule a presentation...
at your church or organization, please email us at:

Counseling4Christians@gmail.com

Personal Study Version

GODLY COUNSEL

Scriptures For Today's World

Written by…

Dr. Brian Campbell

In Collaboration with…

Rev. Jim Angelakos

Acknowledgements

A special thanks to Rev. Jim Angelakos for his help and encouragement throughout this project.

To my father and mother, who dedicated their lives to me, and who raised my brother and me in a Godly household.

Copyright

Copyright 2010, by Dr. Brian Campbell
(All Rights Reserved (Revised Edition))

Scriptures taken from the Holy Bible,
New International Version®, NIV®.
Copyright © 1973, 1978, 1984 by Biblica, Inc.™
Used by permission of Zondervan.
All rights reserved worldwide.
www.zondervan.com

Note: In this book, the words of Christ are printed in italics. Consistent with modern editing practices, beginning and ending ellipses have been omitted when only partial quotes of Scriptures have been utilized. Also, quotation marks have been omitted except where they were necessary for clarity. Because of these editing practices, please always consult the original biblical text before quoting any Scriptures in this book.

Contents

Foreword: This Book is About God's Word   7

Lesson:

1. Abortion   9
2. Addictions   15
3. Adolescent Rebellion   24
4. Anger   31
5. Anxiety/Worry/Fear   39
6. Backsliding   43
7. Belief/Salvation   53
8. Christ, Who He Is   62
9. Citizenship   66
10. Communication   70
11. Death and Dying   83
12. Depression   91
13. Divorce   104
14. Forgive/Forgiveness   108
15. Grief   112
16. Judgmental   116
17. Love   121
18. Marriage   132
19. Money/Riches   136
20. Parenting   140
21. Persecution   146
22. Prayer   151
23. Pride   167
24. Self-Esteem, Low   171
25. Sexual Sin   181
26. Sin   188
27. Suffering   197
28. Temptation   204
29. Thinking, Healthy   214
30. Trouble/Hardship   219
31. Truth   223
32. Unemployment   229
33. Weak/Tired   235

Topical Index: 239

For our children and grandchildren,

**"*Anyone can count the seeds in an apple,
but only God can count the number of apples in a seed.*"**
(Robert Schuller)

Pass it on....

(9-12.15.22.5-25.15.21: 13.1.3.11.5.14.26.9.5; 3.1.12.5.2; 8.5.14.18.25; 2.1.2.25)

Foreword

This Book Is About God's Word

The Word of God is living and active and relevant to today's world and to today's problems. There is no greater authority for Christian living than God's Holy Word.

Whatever your problem, concern, or question may be, God has provided valuable guidance and counsel in the Bible. This book is a follow-up and companion to a previous book authored by Dr. Campbell entitled: "Pearls: Scriptures To Live By."

"Pearls" grew out of Dr. Campbell's work as a Christian psychologist. It consists of over 2,500 Scriptures for counsel and guidance, compiled under 172 topics relevant to Christian mental health.

The idea for the current work, "Godly Counsel," was first suggested by Rev. Jim Angelakos, who saw a need for a "Synopsis" (summary) of topics covered in "Pearls." Many of the subjects covered in "Pearls" are synthesized and subsumed under the major headings in "Godly Counsel."

Focus On The Scriptures

This book is primarily about Scriptures—how they speak to mental health issues prevalent in our society. As you read the "Synopsis" for each chapter, take time to read the Scriptures that relate to the summary text. The Scriptures are conveniently located at the bottom of each page.

Please take time to read the Scriptures supporting the text.

The Scriptures will change your thinking, and ultimately change your life.

Topical Index

If you do not see your problem/concern among the major "Lessons" included in this book, please consult the **Topical Index** (p. 239).

Lesson 1

Abortion

"For you created my inmost being; you knit me
together in my mother's womb."
(Psalm 130:13)

Abortion: termination of pregnancy
or fetal development

The term "abortion" does not appear in the Bible. However, the Bible contains numerous passages that relate to the topic of "life before birth" and God's special relationship with the unborn child. If you are contemplating an abortion, you should consider these Scriptures carefully. If you have had an abortion, the Bible points to God's abiding love and forgiveness for all those who repent.

Synopsis

Almighty God is the creator of all things,[1] including all human life.[2,3] We exist, because He exists.[4] A mother's womb is not a secret place to our heavenly Father; the unborn baby is not hidden

---

For you created all things, and by your will they were
created and have their being.
(Revelation 4:11)[1]

The LORD God formed the man from the dust of the ground
and breathed into his nostrils the breath of life, and the
man became a living being.
(Genesis 2:7)[2]

In his hand is the life of every creature
and the breath of all mankind.
(Job 12:10)[3]

For in him we live and move and have our being.
(Acts 17:28)[4]

from God's sight.[5] The creation of human life from the union of egg and sperm is a miraculous process made possible by God's creative power.[6]

Human beings are made in God's image.[7] From the moment of conception, and throughout the entire nine months of prenatal development, God's hands form us and mold us according to the purposes He has planned for us in life.[8-12] Without question, God is actively and intimately involved in the formation of babies from the point of conception until birth.[13]

> My frame was not hidden from you when I was made in the secret place. When I was woven together in the depths of the earth, your eyes saw my unformed body. All the days ordained for me were written in your book before one of them came to be.
> **(Psalm 139:15-16)**[5]

> For from him and through him and to him are all things. To him be the glory forever! Amen.
> **(Romans 11:36)**[6]

> So God created man in his own image, in the image of God he created him; male and female he created them.
> **(Genesis 1:27)**[7]

> For you created my inmost being; you knit me together in my mother's womb. I praise you because I am fearfully and wonderfully made; your works are wonderful, I know that full well.
> **(Psalm 139:13-14)**[8]

> Your hands shaped me and made me...You gave me life and showed me kindness.
> **(Job 10:8,12)**[9]

> We are the clay, you are the potter; we are all the work of your hand.
> **(Isaiah 64:8)**[10]

> Listen to me, O house of Jacob, all you who remain of the house of Israel, you whom I have upheld since you were conceived...I have made you and I will carry you; I will sustain you and I will rescue you.
> **(Isaiah 46:3-4)**[11]

> Did not he who made me in the womb make them? Did not the same one form us both within our mothers?
> **(Job 31:15)**[12]

Jesus Christ, our Lord and Savior, went through the process of human development in His mother's womb, just like all other babies in the history of mankind. Following His miraculous conception through the Holy Spirit,[14] Jesus grew as an unborn baby in Mary's womb until she gave birth to Him in Bethlehem.[15] From the point of conception onward, Jesus was fully human and fully God. The history of Jesus' life on earth begins at the point of conception.

The word "fetus" does not appear in the Bible. Instead, the unborn baby in the womb is referred to as a "baby,"[16] "child,"[17] or "infant."[18] These terms imply the existence of a separate human being. For example, when Mary became pregnant with Jesus, she was said to be "with ***child***."[17] Using similar terminology, the prophet Job referred to a stillborn baby who died before birth as an "***infant***" who never saw the light of day."[18]

At certain stages of development, it is clear that babies in the womb perceive their environment, are capable of movement independent of their mothers, and experience emotions. While Mary

---

This is what the LORD says—he who made you, who formed you in the womb.
(Isaiah 44:2)[13]

This is how the birth of Jesus Christ came about: His mother Mary was pledged to be married to Joseph, but before they came together, she was found to be with child through the Holy Spirit.
(Matthew 1:18)[14]

While they were there, the time came for the baby [Jesus] to be born, and she gave birth to her first-born, a son.
(Luke 2:6-7)[15]

When Elizabeth heard Mary's greeting, the baby leaped in her womb, and Elizabeth was filled with the Holy Spirit.
(Luke 1:41)[16]

Mary, you have found favor with God. You will be with child and give birth to a son, and you are to give him the name Jesus.
(Luke 1:30-31)[17]

Or why was I not hidden in the ground like a stillborn child, like an infant who never saw the light of day?
(Job 3:16)[18]

was still pregnant with Jesus, she visited her sister, Elizabeth, who was also pregnant with a son who would be named John the Baptist. When Elizabeth heard Mary's greeting, the baby (John the Baptist) "leaped for joy," in his mother's womb when he came into the presence of Jesus.[19]

The mother's womb is sacred; God sometimes assigns a very special role to babies while they are still in the womb. For example, before the prophet Jeremiah was born, while he was still in his mother's womb, he was appointed by God to be a prophet to the nations.[20] The prophet Isaiah also received his calling before he was born—while still being formed by God in his mother's womb.[21]

The Bible condemns murder[22] and the killing of the innocent.[23] The Tenth Commandment proclaims: "Thou shall not murder."[24] The Lord hates "hands that shed innocent blood."[25]

As soon as the sound of your greeting reached my ears, the baby in my womb leaped for joy.
(Luke 1:44)[19]

Before I formed you in the womb I knew you, before you were born I set you apart; I appointed you as a prophet to the nations.
(Jeremiah 1:5)[20]

Before I was born the LORD called me; from my birth he has made mention of my name...And now the LORD says—he who formed me in the womb to be his servant...
(Isaiah 49:1,5)[21]

Jesus replied, *"Do not murder."*
(Matthew 19:18)[22]

Have nothing to do with a false charge, and do not put an innocent or honest person to death, for I will not acquit the guilty.
(Exodus 23:7)[23]

You shall not murder.
(Exodus 20:13)[24]

There are six things the LORD hates...hands that shed innocent blood.
(Proverbs 6:16,17)[25]

God's Guidance

Abortions are typically "secret" endeavors; but nothing in all creation is hidden from God's sight.[26] He is aware of all we do and considers whether our actions are good or evil.[27,28] Without the redemptive sacrifice of Jesus Christ on the cross, God would bring every deed into judgment, including every hidden thing that we have done.[29,30]

Fortunately, if we believe in Jesus and repent of our sins, forgiveness is possible for all sins, even abortion.[31,32] Once we confess

> Nothing in all creation is hidden from God's sight.
> Everything is uncovered and laid bare before the
> eyes of him to whom we must give account.
> **(Psalm 94:9)**[26]
>
> From heaven the LORD looks down and sees all mankind;
> from his dwelling place he watches all who live on
> earth—he who forms the hearts of all,
> who considers everything they do.
> **(Psalm 33:13-15)**[27]
>
> My eyes are on all their ways; they are not hidden from me,
> nor is their sin concealed from my eyes.
> **(Jeremiah 16:17)**[28]
>
> For we must all appear before the judgment seat of Christ,
> that each one may receive what is due him for the things
> done while in the body, whether good or bad.
> **(2 Corinthians 5:10)**[29]
>
> God demonstrates his love for us in this: While we were
> still sinners, Christ died for us.
> **(Romans 5:8)**[30]
>
> Everyone who believes in him receives forgiveness of
> sins through his name.
> **(Acts 10:43)**[31]
>
> If we confess our sins, he is faithful and just and will forgive
> us our sins and purify us from all unrighteousness.
> **(1 John 1:9)**[32]

our sins and are forgiven, our sins are never counted against us.[33] They are removed "as far as the east is from the west."[34] Once forgiven, God does not even remember our sins any more.[35]

The main theme of the Bible is God's unfailing love for us, His children, whom He created.[36] He loved us so much he sent His only Son to die for us.[37] Because He first loved us,[38] we are to love one another deeply from the heart.[39] We are to do unto others what we would have others do unto us.[40] These commands are vitally important and relevant when considering the act of abortion.

God was reconciling the world to himself in Christ, not counting men's sins against them.
(2 Corinthians 5:19)[33]

As far as the east is from the west, so far has he removed our transgressions from us.
(Psalm 103:12)[34]

Their sins and lawless acts I will remember no more.
(Hebrews 10:17)[35]

My command is this: Love each other as I have loved you.
(John 15:12)[36]

For God so loved the world that he gave his one and only Son, that whoever believes in him shall not perish but have eternal life.
(John 3:16)[37]

Dear friends, since God so loved us, we also ought to love one another.
(1 John 4:11)[38]

Love one another deeply, from the heart.
(1 Peter 1:22)[39]

So in everything, do to others what you would have them do to you, for this sums up the Law and the Prophets.
(Matthew 7:12)[40]

Lesson 2

Addictions

"A man is a slave to whatever has mastered him."
(2 Peter 2:19)

Addiction: being physically or psychologically enslaved to a mood altering habit or practice

Addictions come in many varieties. Our society is riddled with: alcoholism, illicit drugs, prescription drug abuse, gambling, sexual addiction, pornography, cigarette smoking, and food addiction. All of these addictions share one thing in common—they bring temporary pleasure at the expense of long-term, harmful consequences.

Synopsis

Alcoholism: People who drink too much alcohol often ruin their own lives and the lives of those around them; their world is full of strife and sorrow.[1] When a person drinks alcohol, it can go down smoothly at first, but in the end it "bites like a snake and poisons like a viper."[2] Getting drunk leads to a life focused on sensual pleasure (debauchery).[3]

Who has woe? Who has sorrow? Who has strife? Who has complaints? Who has needless bruises? Who has bloodshot eyes? Those who linger over wine, who go to sample bowls of mixed wine.
(Proverbs 23: 29-30)[1]

Do not gaze at wine when it is red, when it sparkles in the cup, when it goes down smoothly! In the end it bites like a snake and poisons like a viper.
(Proverbs 23: 31-32)[2]

Do not get drunk on wine, which leads to debauchery. Instead, be filled with the Spirit.
(Ephesians 5:18)[3]

People who drink alcohol often brag about how much they can drink.[4] They stay up late drinking and then when they wake up they want to drink again.[5] They ridicule others (mock them) and often get into fights.[6] In the end, alcohol consumption can lead to a life of poverty.[7] Most importantly, people who live a lifestyle of drunkenness and lasciviousness place themselves in danger of losing the biggest prize of all—the kingdom of God.[8]

Gluttony: For people who eat too much, their "god" is their stomach; they have their minds set on earthly things.[9] Like the drunkard, gluttons often end up becoming poor because of their overindulgence.[10] The Bible warns us that a companion of gluttons "disgraces his father."[11]

> Woe to those who are heroes at drinking wine
> and champions at mixing drinks.
> **(Isaiah 5:22)**[4]

> Woe to those who rise early in the morning to run after their drinks, who stay up late at night till they are inflamed with wine.
> **(Isaiah 5:11)**[5]

> Wine is a mocker and beer a brawler;
> whoever is led astray by them is not wise.
> **(Proverbs 20:1)**[6]

> He who loves pleasure will become poor;
> whoever loves wine and oil will never be rich.
> **(Proverbs 21:17)**[7]

> The acts of the sinful nature are obvious: sexual immorality, impurity and debauchery; idolatry and witchcraft; hatred, discord, jealousy, fits of rage, selfish ambition, dissensions, factions and envy; drunkenness, orgies, and the like. I warn you, as I did before, that those who live like this will not inherit the kingdom of God.
> **(Galatians 5:19-21)**[8]

> Their destiny is destruction, their god is their stomach, and their glory is in their shame. Their mind is on earthly things.
> **(Philippians 3:19)**[9]

> Do not join those who drink too much wine or gorge themselves on meat, for drunkards and gluttons become poor, and drowsiness clothes them in rags.
> **(Proverbs 23:20-21)**[10]

Drug Addiction: Drug addicts abuse their bodies. Such abuse is offensive to God, because our bodies are God's temple and the Holy Spirit lives in us.[12,13] Anyone who destroys God's sacred temple, God will destroy him.[13]

Drug addicts are slaves to their drugs and controlled by their sinful nature.[14,15] Living according to the sinful nature leads to death, but living according to the Spirit leads to life. Those who live by the sinful nature cannot please God.[16,17] God wants us to purify ourselves from everything that contaminates the body and spirit, "perfecting holiness out of reverence for God."[18]

Sexual Addiction: People who are sexually addicted have a craving for more and more sex, often in increasingly perverted ways.

He who keeps the law is a discerning son, but a companion of gluttons disgraces his father.
(Proverbs 28:7)[11]

For we are the temple of the living God.
(2 Corinthians 6:16)[12]

Don't you know that you yourselves are God's temple and that God's Spirit lives in you? If anyone destroys God's temple, God will destroy him; for God's temple is sacred, and you are that temple.
(1 Corinthians 3:16-17)[13]

A man is a slave to whatever has mastered him.
(2 Peter 2:19)[14]

Everyone who sins is a slave to sin. Now a slave has no permanent place in the family, but a son belongs to it forever.
(John 8:34-35)[15]

Those controlled by the sinful nature cannot please God.
(Romans 8:8)[16]

For if you live according to the sinful nature, you will die; but if by the Spirit you put to death the misdeeds of the body, you will live, because those who are led by the Spirit of God are sons of God.
(Romans 8:13-14)[17]

Let us purify ourselves from everything that contaminates body and spirit, perfecting holiness out of reverence for God.
(2 Corinthians 7:1)[18]

The men and women of Sodom and Gomorrah and ancient Rome became preoccupied with sex, with a continual lust for more.[19,20] Both these civilizations perished.

As Christians, we are to abstain from sexual immorality; all other sins a man commits are outside his body, but he who sins sexually sins against his own body.[21] We are to learn to control our bodies in a way that is holy and honorable, not in passionate lust like the people who do not know God.[22]

We are to "put to death" sexual immorality and impurity and everything that belongs to our earthly nature.[23] We are to get rid of all moral filth.[24] Your body is a "temple of the Holy Spirit," who is in you, and which you have received from God. Therefore, you can't

---

Sodom and Gomorrah and the surrounding towns gave themselves up to sexual immorality and perversion. They serve as an example of those who suffer the punishment of eternal fire.
(Jude 1:7)[19]

Having lost all sensitivity, they have given themselves over to sensuality so as to indulge in every kind of impurity, with a continual lust for more.
(Ephesians 4:19)[20]

Flee from sexual immorality. All other sins a man commits are outside his body, but he who sins sexually sins against his own body.
(1 Corinthians 6:18)[21]

It is God's will that you should be sanctified: that you should avoid sexual immorality; that each of you should learn to control his own body in a way that is holy and honorable, not in passionate lust like the heathen, who do not know God; and that in this matter no one should wrong his brother or take advantage of him.
(1 Thessalonians 4:3-5)[22]

Put to death, therefore, whatever belongs to your earthly nature: sexual immorality, impurity, lust, evil desires and greed, which is idolatry.
(Colossians 3:5)[23]

Therefore, get rid of all moral filth and the evil that is so prevalent and humbly accept the word planted in you.
(James 1:21)[24]

just do whatever you want to do with your body. It was bought for a price—Christ's death on the cross. Therefore, you are to honor God with your body.[25]

People with sexual addictions often take advantage of other people to meet their desires; this runs contrary to God's teaching. We should treat others with "absolute purity,"[26] without even a hint of sexual immorality.[27] God has a dire warning for those who live a lifestyle of willful and unrepentant sexual sin—they will not inherit the kingdom of God.[28]

Gambling Addiction: The Bible warns us to keep ourselves free of the love of money and to be content with what we have.[29] People who want to get rich quickly, get trapped in their sin and do many foolish and harmful things that end up in "ruin and destruction."[30] The love of money is the root of all kinds of evil.[31]

> Do you not know that your body is a temple of the Holy Spirit, who is in you, whom you have received from God? You are not your own; you were bought at a price. Therefore honor God with your body.
> **(1 Corinthians 6:19-20)**[25]

> Treat younger men as brothers, older women as mothers, and younger women as sisters, with absolute purity.
> **(1 Timothy 5:1-2)**[26]

> But among you there must not be even a hint of sexual immorality, or of any kind of impurity, or of greed, because these are improper for God's holy people.
> **(Ephesians 5:3)**[27]

> Do you not know that the wicked will not inherit the kingdom of God? Do not be deceived: Neither the sexually immoral nor idolaters nor adulterers nor male prostitutes nor homosexual offenders nor thieves nor the greedy nor drunkards nor slanderers nor swindlers will inherit the kingdom of God.
> **(1 Corinthians 6:9-11)**[28]

> Keep your lives free from the love of money and be content with what you have.
> **(Hebrews 13:5)**[29]

> People who want to get rich fall into temptation and a trap and into many foolish and harmful desires that plunge men into ruin and destruction.
> **(1 Timothy 6:9)**[30]

People who love money never seem to have enough.[32] People who gamble want to "get rich quick," but the Bible warns us not to wear ourselves out trying to get rich.[33] The person who chases fantasies of being wealthy will end up with "his fill of poverty,"[34] and anyone eager to get rich "will not go unpunished."[35]

God's Guidance

People who are "hooked" on the short-term pleasure of addictions find it extremely difficult to break their habits. They become slaves to their sin.[36,37] Time after time they have tried to resist, but time after time they have given in to temptation.[38-40] Only God offers an effective "way out" of addictions.

For the love of money is the root of all kinds of evil.
(1 Timothy 6:10)[31]

Whoever loves money never has money enough.
(Ecclesiastes 5:10)[32]

Do not wear yourselves out trying to get rich; have the wisdom to show restraint.
(Proverbs 23:4)[33]

He who works his land will have abundant food, but the one who chases fantasies will have his fill of poverty.
(Proverbs 28:19)[34]

A faithful man will be richly blessed, but one eager to get rich will not go unpunished.
(Proverbs 28:20)[35]

A man is a slave to whatever has mastered him.
(2 Peter 2:19)[36]

I tell you the truth, everyone who sins is a slave to sin.
(John 8:34)[37]

I do not understand what I do. For what I want to do I do not do, but what I hate I do.
(Romans 7:15)[38]

For what I do is not the good I want to do; no, the evil I do not want to do—this I keep on doing.
(Romans 7:19)[39]

All addictions represent a battle between what the flesh wants and what the spirit desires.[41] The first step in overcoming addictions is to recognize that you cannot control your addiction on your own—you need God's help. Remember that God will never let you be tempted beyond what you can bear,[42] and when you are tempted He will always provide a way out, so that you can "stand up" under the temptation.[43]

If you are addicted, turn to God.[44] If you confess with your mouth "Jesus is Lord," and believe in your heart that God raised Him from the dead, you will receive eternal salvation.[45] You will become an entirely new creation and will be "born again," and filled with the

---

> I know that nothing good lives in me, that is, in my sinful nature. For I have the desire to do what is good, but I cannot carry it out.
> **(Romans 7:18)**[40]
>
> So I say, live by the Spirit, and you will not gratify the desires of the sinful nature. For the sinful nature desires what is contrary to the spirit, and the spirit what is contrary to the sinful nature.
> **(Galatians 5:16-17)**[41]
>
> And God is faithful; he will not let you be tempted beyond what you can bear.
> **(1 Corinthians 10:13)**[42]
>
> But when you are tempted, he will also provide a way out so that you can stand up under it.
> **(1 Corinthians 10:13)**[43]
>
> What a wretched man I am! Who will rescue me from this body of death? Thanks be to God—through Jesus Christ our Lord!
> **(Romans 7:24-25)**[44]
>
> That if you confess with your mouth, "Jesus is Lord," and believe in your heart that God raised him from the dead, you will be saved.
> **(Romans 10:9)**[45]

Holy Spirit, the great Counselor.[46] You will no longer be controlled by the sinful nature, but by the Spirit of God, who lives in you.[47,48]

Live one day at a time, and pray each day that God will take away your sinful desire.[49] Completely abandon yourself to God, and seek His will for your life.[50] Fix your eyes on Jesus, the author and perfecter of our faith.[51] "Clothe yourselves with the Lord Jesus Christ," and stop thinking about how to gratify the desires of your addiction.[52]

In humility, regularly confess your sins to God,[53] and to your fellow man.[54] Seek out anyone you may have harmed because of your

---

But the Counselor, the Holy Spirit, whom the Father will send in my name, will teach you all things and will remind you of everything I have said to you.
(John 14:26)[46]

You, however, are controlled not by the sinful nature but by the Spirit, if the Spirit of God lives in you.
(Romans 8:9)[47]

For if you live according to the sinful nature, you will die; but if by the spirit you put to death the misdeeds of the body, you will live, because those who are led by the Spirit of God are sons of God.
(Romans 8:13-14)[48]

I tell you the truth, my father will give you anything you ask in my name.
(John 16:23)[49]

The world and its desires pass away, but the man who does the will of God lives forever.
(1 John 2:17)[50]

Let us fix our eyes on Jesus, the author and perfecter of our faith.
(Hebrews 12:2)[51]

Clothe yourselves with the Lord Jesus Christ, and do not think about how to gratify the desires of the sinful nature.
(Romans 13:14)[52]

If we confess our sins, he is faithful and just and will forgive us our sins and purify us from all unrighteousness.
(1 John 1:9)[53]

addiction and ask for forgiveness. Forgive yourself also, for we are all sinners and have fallen short of the glory of God.[55] Remember, God showed His love for us by this: "While were still sinners, Christ died for us."[56]

Always have hope.[57] Even though you are not strong enough to conquer your addiction by yourself, with God's help you can.[58] And if the Son of God sets you free, "you will be free indeed."[59]

Finally, once God has delivered you from your addiction, go and tell others who may also be suffering,[60] so that they too may have hope and come to a knowledge of God's mighty power and authority over sin.

> Confess your sins to each other and pray for each other
> so that you may be healed.
> **(James 5:16)**[54]
>
> For all have sinned and fall short of the glory of God.
> **(Romans 3:23)**[55]
>
> But God demonstrates his own love for us in this:
> While we were still sinners, Christ died for us.
> **(Romans 5:8)**[56]
>
> Anyone who is among the living has hope.
> **(Ecclesiastes 9:4)**[57]
>
> Jesus looked at them and said, *"With man this is impossible,*
> *but with God all things are possible."*
> **(Matthew 19:26)**[58]
>
> *So if the Son sets you free,*
> *you will be free indeed.*
> **(John 8:36)**[59]
>
> Blessed are those who have learned to acclaim you,
> who walk in the light of your presence, O Lord.
> **(Psalm 89:15)**[60]

Lesson 3

Adolescent Rebellion

"Listen, my son, to your father's instruction and do
not forsake your mother's teaching."
(Proverbs 1:8)

Rebellion: an act of defiance toward those
who are in authority or in control

Adolescents are under tremendous pressure in today's society. Premarital sex, drugs, gangs, pornography, and a host of other societal ills threaten to win them over into sinful lives and destruction. As parents, we sometimes feel helpless and overwhelmed and don't know where to turn. Fortunately, the Bible is a great source of wisdom and guidance for raising adolescents. Bottom line, the best thing you can do to raise healthy and God-fearing children is to train them in God's Word, keep them away from bad influences, and teach them to obey and respect your authority through love and discipline.

Synopsis

Parents are commanded to take an active role in training their children.[1] They need to teach their adolescents God's Word and introduce them to the powerful advice and counsel that God provides for young people. The Bible is not just for adults. God speaks directly to young people on numerous occasions.

So listen closely adolescents! Here is some sound advice you would be wise to follow...

Train a child in the way he should go and when he is old
he will not turn from it.
(Proverbs 22:6)[1]

Even a child is known by his actions, by whether his
conduct is pure and right.
(Proverbs 20:11)[2]

Set An Example for Others: Just because you are a young person doesn't mean that you can "get away" with bad behavior and not be accountable. Even the actions of children are judged according to whether they are pure and right.[2] Young people are instructed to set a good example for other believers.[3] How you live your lives is extremely important!

Parents and adults are told not to look down on you just because you are young.[3] In fact, God wants to use you to set an example for adults and other Christians in terms of how you live your life, how you talk to other people, how you love others, your faith, and your purity.[3]

So, never think that what you do as a young person doesn't matter or will be excused by God because you are young. God wants you to be happy and follow your heart,[4] but remember that everything you do—even the things you do as a young person—will ultimately be brought into judgment (for rewards if you are saved, and for punishment if you are not saved).[4]

Listen to Instruction: If your parents are "God-fearing" Christians who teach you the Bible, you should listen to their advice and accept their instruction.[5] You will be wise if you do,[6,7] and

---

> Don't let anyone look down on you because you are young, but set an example for the believers in speech, in life, in love, in faith, and in purity.
> **(1 Timothy 4:12)**[3]
>
> Be happy, young man, while you are young, and let your heart give you joy in the days of your youth. Follow the ways of your heart and whatever your eyes see, but know that for all these things God will bring you to judgment.
> **(Ecclesiastes 11:9)**[4]
>
> Listen, my son, to your father's instruction and do not forsake your mother's teaching.
> **(Proverbs 1:8)**[5]
>
> Listen to advice and accept instruction, and in the end you will be wise.
> **(Proverbs 19:20)**[6]
>
> A wise son heeds his father's instruction, but a mocker does not listen to rebuke.
> **(Proverbs 13:1)**[7]

the knowledge you gain will be important to you throughout your lifetime.[8] If you don't follow your parents' instructions, bad things often happen[9] and at the end of your life, you may look back and wish that you had listened to what they told you.[10]

Obey Your Parents: Once again, if your parents are Christians and being Christ-like in their actions, you should try to obey everything they tell you to do.[11,12] The Lord says He is pleased when you do this.[11] Stop rebelling and arguing over every little thing; submit your will to your parents' will and try to live the kind of life they are training you to live.[13]

Keep Good Company: No matter how well your parents have trained you in the truth, and no matter how often you have been to church or Sunday school, be careful with whom you associate. If you allow yourself to associate with "bad company,"[14,15] or young people who are rebelling against authority and against society,[16] you are putting yourself at risk.

Hold on to instruction, do not let it go;
guard it well, for it is your life.
(Proverbs 4:13)[8]

He who scorns instruction will pay for it, but he
who respects a command is rewarded.
(Proverbs 13:13)[9]

At the end of your life you will groan, when your flesh and body are spent. You will say, "How I hated discipline! How my heart spurned correction! I would not obey my teachers or listen to my instructors. I have come to the brink of utter ruin in the midst of the whole assembly."
(Proverbs 5:11-14)[10]

Children, obey your parents in everything,
for this pleases the Lord.
(Colossians 3:20)[11]

Children, obey your parents in the Lord, for this is right.
(Ephesians 6:1)[12]

My son, give me your heart
and let your eyes keep to my ways.
(Proverbs 23:26)[13]

Do not be misled: "Bad company corrupts good character."
(1 Corinthians 15:33)[14]

Just because you think you have good morals and couldn't possibly be led astray, don't fool yourself! King Solomon, one of the wisest men who ever lived, said that "He who walks with the wise grows wise, but a companion of fools suffers harm."[17] If King Solomon met your friends, would he think they were foolish or wise? If your so-called "friends" try to coax you into sin, don't give in to them.[18] Better yet, find some different friends!

Accept Discipline: Most young people hate discipline. It's hard for them to understand that discipline is actually a sign of love. The Bible clearly states that God Himself disciplines those He loves, just as a father disciplines the son he loves.[19] If you ignore the discipline that your parents give you, and don't learn from it, you are really only hurting yourself,[20] and being foolish.[21]

A Final Note: Sometimes it doesn't seem possible to live like a Christian in today's society. There are so many pressures and so

---

Do not set foot on the path of the wicked or
walk in the way of evil men.
(Proverbs 4:14)[15]

Fear the LORD and the king, my son,
and do not join with the rebellious.
(Proverbs 24:21)[16]

He who walks with the wise grows wise,
but a companion of fools suffers harm.
(Proverbs 13:20)[17]

My son, if sinners entice you,
do not give in to them.
(Proverbs 1:10)[18]

My son, do not despise the LORD's discipline and do not
resent his rebuke, because the LORD disciplines those
he loves, as a father the son he delights in.
(Proverbs 3:11-12)[19]

He who ignores discipline despises himself, but whoever
heeds correction gains understanding.
(Proverbs 15:32)[20]

A fool spurns his father's discipline, but whoever
heeds correction shows prudence.
(Proverbs 15:5)[21]

many temptations. However, God promises that there is a way to make it through—by living according to His Word,[22] and by honoring your father and mother.[23]

God's Guidance

God wants us to be obedient to our parents, but He also wants us to be obedient to Him.[24-26] We show our love for God when we obey His commands (as found in the Holy Scriptures) and follow the instructions He gives for us in the Bible.[27,28]

> How can a young man keep his way pure? By living according to your word.
> **(Psalm 119:9)**[22]

> Honor your father and mother...that it may go well with you and that you may enjoy long life on the earth.
> **(Ephesians 6:2)**[23]

> Walk in the ways I command you, that it may go well with you.
> **(Jeremiah 7:23)**[24]

> Obey me and do everything I command you, and you will be my people, and I will be your God.
> **(Jeremiah 11:4)**[25]

> *Why do you call me, 'Lord, Lord,' and do not do what I say?*
> **(Luke 6:46)**[26]

> This is love for God: to obey his commands.
> **(1 John 5:3)**[26]

> If you love me, you will obey what I command.
> **(John 14:15)**[27]

> If you obey my commands, you will remain in my love, just as I have obeyed my Father's commands and remain in his love.
> **(John 15:10)**[28]

> I have hidden your word in my heart that I might not sin against you.
> **(Psalm 119:11)**[29]

Unfortunately, many adolescents are stubborn and resist reading God's Word. They can't obey God because they have never taken the time to study the Bible and see how God instructs them to live their lives.

One of the best things you can do to stay out of trouble and live a holy life is to hide God's Word in your heart.[29-31] God's advice is always perfect,[32] flawless,[33] trustworthy,[34] and eternal[35-37]— and He loves it when we follow His commandments.

Reading and memorizing Scriptures will help you resist evil and do what is right. God Himself promises that if we obey His commandments things will always turn out better for us.[38]

When your words came, I ate them; they were my joy and my heart's delight, for I bear your name, O LORD God Almighty.
(Jeremiah 15:16)[30]

I will not neglect your word.
(Psalm 119:16)[31]

The law of the LORD is perfect, reviving the soul.
(Psalm 19:7)[32]

Every word of God is flawless.
(Proverbs 30:5)[33]

The statutes you have laid down are righteous;
they are fully trustworthy.
(Psalm 119:138)[34]

Your word, O LORD, is eternal; it stands firm in the heavens.
(Psalm 119:89)[35]

The grass withers and the flowers fall, but the
word of our God stands forever.
(Isaiah 40:8)[36]

*It is easier for heaven and earth to disappear than for the
least stroke of a pen to drop out of the Law.*
(Luke 16:17)[37]

Oh, that their hearts would be inclined to fear me and keep
all my commands always, so that it might go well with
them and their children forever!
(Deuteronomy 5:29)[38]

So, if you have a choice between "going along" with your friends and being rebellious and sinful, try choosing God's way instead.[39] Remember what you learn in the Bible and what your parents and others teach you about God's Word—and try to obey it![40]

> We must obey God rather than men!
> **(Acts 5:29)**[39]
>
> *Remember, therefore, what you have received and heard; obey it, and repent.*
> **(Revelation 3:3)**[40]

Lesson 4

Anger

"Do not be quickly provoked in your spirit,
for anger resides in the lap of fools."
(Ecclesiastes 7:9)

Anger: a strong feeling of displeasure, hostility,
or antagonism towards someone or something,
usually combined with an urge to harm

God gets angry with human beings when they don't follow His commandments and when they are sinful and rebellious. Jesus Christ displayed "righteous anger," and this is the only form of anger acceptable for man to express. Other forms of anger are unacceptable, and are admonished throughout the Scriptures.

Synopsis

God's Anger: The Lord our God is gracious, loving, forgiving, and compassionate.[1] He is slow to anger and rich in love.[2] However, when God is provoked sufficiently, His anger can be fierce.[3,4] For example, He destroyed the city of Sodom and Gomorrah because

---

The LORD, the LORD, the compassionate and gracious God, slow
to anger, abounding in love and faithfulness, maintaining love
to thousands, and forgiving wickedness, rebellion and sin.
(Exodus 34:6-7)[1]

"The LORD is slow to anger, abounding in love and
forgiving sin and rebellion."
(Numbers 14:18)[2]

Who knows the power of your anger? For your wrath is
as great as the fear that is due you.
(Psalm 90:11)[3]

God's anger rose against them; he put to death the sturdiest
among them, cutting down the young men of Israel.
(Psalm 78:31)[4]

of their evil ways,[5] and His anger "burned" against the pharaoh when he would not let the Jewish people leave Egypt.[6]

God is a jealous God, and He gets angry when His people worship idols or other "gods," and when they forsake Him.[7-9] If we reject God's Word, as contained in the Bible, and fail to follow His commandments, we should properly fear God's anger and wrath.[10] Fortunately, if we obey God's commands, humble ourselves before Him, and seek righteousness, we can shield ourselves from His anger.[11]

> The whole land will be a burning waste of salt and sulfur—nothing planted, nothing sprouting, no vegetation growing on it. It will be like the destruction of Sodom and Gomorrah, Admah and Zeboiim, which the LORD overthrew in fierce anger.
> **(Deuteronomy 29:23)**[5]

> Therefore the LORD's anger burned against this land, so that he brought on it all the curses written in this book.
> **(Deuteronomy 29:27)**[6]

> They made him jealous with their foreign gods and angered him with their detestable idols.
> **(Deuteronomy 32:16)**[7]

> If you forsake the LORD and serve foreign gods, he will turn and bring disaster on you and make an end of you, after he has been good to you.
> **(Joshua 24:20)**[8]

> The gracious hand of our God is on everyone who looks to him, but his great anger is against all who forsake him."
> **(Ezra 8:22)**[9]

> Great is the LORD's anger that burns against us because our fathers have not obeyed the words of this book; they have not acted in accordance with all that is written there concerning us.
> **(2 Kings 22:13)**[10]

> Seek the LORD, all you humble of the land, you who do what he commands. Seek righteousness, seek humility; perhaps you will be sheltered on the day of the LORD's anger.
> **(Zephaniah 2:3)**[11]

Christ's Righteous Anger: Jesus Christ showed anger when He drove the moneychangers out of the temple.[12] He also got angry when people doubted that He could heal a man's hand,[13] and when the Pharisees were being hypocritical.[14] These were instances of "righteous anger."

Man's Righteous Anger/Rebuke: Righteous anger is the only kind of anger that God permits for human beings, and even when we engage in this type of anger, we must be careful that we do not "cross over the line" and sin.[15] Whenever possible, we should rebuke our fellow man frankly,[16] but gently,[17] remembering our own

---

Jesus entered the temple area and drove out all who were buying and selling there. He overturned the tables of the money changers and the benches of those selling doves. *"It is written,"* he said to them, *"My house will be called a house of prayer, but you are making it a den of robbers."*
(Matthew 21:12-13)[12]

He looked around at them in anger and, deeply distressed at their stubborn hearts, said to the man, *"Stretch out your hand."* He stretched it out, and his hand was completely restored.
(Mark 3:5)[13]

"Woe to you, teachers of the law and Pharisees, you hypocrites! You are like whitewashed tombs, which look beautiful on the outside but on the inside are full of dead men's bones and everything unclean."
(Matthew 23:27)[14]

"In your anger do not sin": Do not let the sun go down while you are still angry, and do not give the devil a foothold.
(Ephesians 4:26-7)[15]

Rebuke your neighbor frankly so you will not share in his guilt.
(Leviticus 19:17)[16]

Brothers, if someone is caught in a sin, you who are spiritual should restore him gently. But watch yourself, or you also may be tempted.
(Galatians 6:1)[17]

sinful nature and imperfections.[18] We are to correct, rebuke, and encourage "with great patience and careful instruction."[19]

Refrain From Anger: Unfortunately, man's anger is not always "righteous anger," and the Bible advises against most forms of anger.[20] In general, God desires that we refrain from anger[21] and keep ourselves under control.[22] Quick-tempered people often do foolish things,[23,24] and man's anger doesn't bring about the righteous life that God desires.[25]

God's Guidance

Watch What You Say: God wants us to be careful about how we talk to others.[26,27] Jesus reminds us that all men will have to give

---

There is not a righteous man on earth who does what is right and never sins.
(Ecclesiastes 7:20)[18]

Preach the Word; be prepared in season and out of season; correct, rebuke and encourage—with great patience and careful instruction.
(2 Timothy 4:2)[19]

Get rid of all bitterness, rage and anger, brawling and slander, along with every form of malice.
(Ephesians 4:31)[20]

Refrain from anger and turn from wrath.
(Psalm 37:8)[21]

A fool gives full vent to his anger, but a wise man keeps himself under control.
(Proverbs 29:11)[22]

A quick-tempered man does foolish things.
(Proverbs 14:17)[23]

Do not be quickly provoked in your spirit, for anger resides in the lap of fools.
(Ecclesiastes 7:9)[24]

Everyone should be quick to listen, slow to speak and slow to become angry, for man's anger does not bring about the righteous life that God desires.
(James 1:19-20)[25]

an account on the day of judgment for every careless word they have spoken.[28] Reckless words can "pierce like a sword," and can do significant harm to others.[29]

Control Yourself: When provoked, try to remain calm and avoid shouting.[30] Step back and think about what you are going to say before you say it, and don't speak in haste.[31] Often, you can calm a quarrel by remaining quiet and being patient.[30-33] Remember that a "gentle answer" can defuse a situation and stop an argument from getting out of control.[34] In fact, if you control your

---

> He who guards his lips guards his life, but he who speaks rashly will come to ruin.
> **(Proverbs 13:3)**[26]
>
> The tongue has the power of life and death.
> **(Proverbs 18:21)**[27]
>
> *But I tell you that men will have to give an account on the day of judgment for every careless word they have spoken.*
> **(Matthew 12:36)**[28]
>
> Reckless words pierce like a sword, but the tongue of the wise brings healing.
> **(Proverbs 12:18)**[29]
>
> The quiet words of the wise are more to be heeded than the shouts of a ruler of fools.
> **(Ecclesiastes 9:17)**[30]
>
> Do you see a man who speaks in haste? There is more hope for a fool than for him.
> **(Proverbs 29:20)**[31]
>
> A hot-tempered man stirs up dissension, but a patient man calms a quarrel.
> **(Proverbs 15:18)**[32]
>
> Through patience a ruler can be persuaded, and a gentle tongue can break a bone.
> **(Proverbs 25:15)**[33]
>
> A gentle answer turns away wrath, but a harsh word stirs up anger.
> **(Proverbs 15:1)**[34]

temper and are patient, your gentle answer can prove to be a major "weapon" against your opponent.[35,36]

Keep Things In Perspective: Avoid foolish and stupid arguments; they only produce quarrels.[37] People who love to quarrel love sin.[38] Keep things in perspective, and learn to drop things that aren't really that important.[39] Don't pay attention to every word that people say[40] and try to "hold your tongue" before speaking;[41] develop good listening skills, and try not to respond without first hearing what the other person has to say.[42]

Don't Go to Bed Angry: If possible, try to resolve your anger with another person before you go to bed at night.[43] This may require

---

Better a patient man than a warrior, a man who controls
his temper than one who takes a city.
(Proverbs 16:32)[35]

Through patience a ruler can be persuaded, and
a gentle tongue can break a bone.
(Proverbs 25:15)[36]

Don't have anything to do with foolish and stupid arguments,
because you know they produce quarrels.
(2 Timothy 2:23)[37]

He who loves a quarrel loves sin.
(Proverbs 17:19)[38]

Starting a quarrel is like breaching a dam; so drop
the matter before a dispute breaks out.
(Proverbs 17:14)[39]

Do not pay attention to every word people say.
(Ecclesiastes 7:21)[40]

He who guards his lips guards his life, but he who
speaks rashly will come to ruin.
(Proverbs 13:3)[41]

He who answers before listening—that is his
folly and his shame.
(Proverbs 18:13)[42]

Do not let the sun go down while you are still angry,
and do not give the devil a foothold.
(Ephesians 4:26-27)[43]

that you forgive the other person, or ask the other person to forgive you.[44] Apparently the devil loves it when we go to bed angry and upset at each other.[43]

Stay Away From Angry People: Anger can be contagious. Scriptures warn us to stay away from people who get angered easily, and avoid making friends with hot-tempered people—so that we don't learn their ways and become angry people ourselves.[45] Hot-tempered people commit many sins,[46] and get into trouble a lot. If you rescue them from their trouble, you will probably have to do it again and again.[47]

Be Wise and Try to Live in Peace: Finally, if you are wise, you will learn to restrain your words[48] and your temper,[49] and turn anger away whenever possible.[50] Never try to stir up anger.[51]

Be kind and compassionate to one another, forgiving each other, just as in Christ God forgave you.
(Ephesians 4:32)[44]

Do not make friends with a hot-tempered man, do not associate with one easily angered, or you may learn his ways and get yourself ensnared.
(Proverbs 22:24-25)[45]

A hot-tempered one [man] commits many sins.
(Proverbs 29:22)[46]

A hot-tempered man must pay the penalty; if you rescue him, you will have to do it again.
(Proverbs 19:19)[47]

A man of knowledge uses words with restraint, and a man of understanding is even-tempered
(Proverbs 17:27)[48]

A fool gives full vent to his anger, but a wise man keeps himself under control.
(Proverbs 29:11)[49]

Wise men turn away anger.
(Proverbs 29:8) [50]

For as churning the milk produces butter, and as twisting the nose produces blood, so stirring up anger produces strife.
(Proverbs 30:33) [51]

Make every effort to live peacefully with all men.[52] Love one another, as God loves us.[53] Remember that love is patient and kind; it keeps no record of wrongs, and it is not easily angered.[54]

> Make every effort to live in peace with all men.
> **(Hebrews 12:14)**[52]
>
> Dear friends, let us love one another,
> for love comes from God.
> **(1 John 4:7)**[53]
>
> Love is patient, love is kind. It does not envy, it does not boast, it is not proud. It is not rude, it is not self-seeking, it is not easily angered, it keeps no record of wrongs.
> **(1 Corinthians 13:4-5)**[54]

Lesson 5

Anxiety/Worry/Fear

"When I am afraid, I will trust in you."
(Psalm 56:3)

Anxiety: an unpleasant state of mental uneasiness or concern
Worry: to feel mentally distressed, anxious, or uneasy
Fear: an anxious feeling caused by the presence of danger

Today's world appears dangerous and unpredictable—reports of wars, earthquakes, disease, poverty, divorce, abortion, and violent crimes, fill our news reports. As a result, people everywhere are feeling overwhelmed with anxiety, worry, and fear. They are afraid they will lose their jobs, their homes, their scholarships, their marriage, their retirement, and a million other things. However, despite the abundance of concerns in our lives, Scriptures tell us that God does not want us to worry or be anxious about ***anything***. In fact, the only thing we are to fear is God alone. The antidote for fear is faith, trust, and love of God.

Synopsis

People who suffer from anxiety and worry tend to focus on the future. They imagine harmful events or catastrophes that may never occur. God's Word tells us that we cannot discover anything about the future.[1] We are to stay in the present and turn all our anxiety over to God because He cares for us.[2] When we give our

> A man cannot discover anything
> about his future.
> **(Ecclesiastes 7:14)**[1]
>
> Cast all your anxiety on him
> because he cares for you.
> **(1 Peter 5:7)**[2]

anxiety to God, He promises that He will sustain us and that He will never let the righteous man fall.[3] We are to cope with today's problems, and not worry about what tomorrow may bring.[4]

In addition to living in the future, people who are anxious tend to "blow things up out of proportion," and worry about this or that little thing. God does not want us to fret about the small stuff.[5] Instead, He wants us to focus on Him,[6] and trust Him for all our needs—even for relatively "big" items like food and clothes.[7] God is well aware that we need these things and promises He will provide.[8]

In the final analysis, God does not want us to be anxious about **anything**,[9] whether in the present or in the future, and whether

---

Cast your cares on the LORD and he will sustain you;
he will never let the righteous fall.
(Psalm 55:22)[3]

Therefore do not worry about tomorrow, for tomorrow will worry about itself. Each day has enough trouble of its own.
(Matthew 6:34)[4]

Do not fret—it leads only to evil.
(Psalm 37:8)[5]

"Martha, Martha," the Lord answered, "you are worried and upset about many things, but only one thing is needed. Mary has chosen what is better, and it will not be taken away from her."
(Luke 10:41-42)[6]

Therefore I tell you, do not worry about your life, what you will eat; or about your body, what you will wear. Life is more than food, and the body more than clothes.
(Luke 12:22-23)[7]

So do not worry, saying "What shall we eat?" or "What shall we drink?" or "What shall we wear?" For the pagans run after all these things, and your heavenly father knows that you need them.
(Matthew 6:31-32)[8]

Do not be anxious about anything, but in everything, by prayer and petition, with thanksgiving, present your requests to God. And the peace of God, which transcends all understanding, will guard your hearts and your minds in Christ Jesus.
(Philippians 4:6-7)[9]

"big" or "small." When we are worried or afraid, He invites us to pray to Him and present our requests to Him. When we do so, He promises He will provide us with peace—peace that is beyond what we can ever understand or grasp.[9]

God's Guidance

God is a loving and powerful Father, who watches over all who love Him.[10] He does not want His children to be fearful or afraid.[11] He instructs us to believe in Him[12] and to trust in Him,[13,14] and He promises that He will watch over us and deliver us from all our fears.[15] He is not a God far away, He is a God nearby.[16]

We do not need to fear natural disasters; God is more powerful than earthquakes and tsunamis.[17] And we do not need to fear

---

The LORD watches over all who love him.
(Psalm 145:20)[10]

Do not be afraid, little flock, for your Father has been pleased to give you the kingdom.
(Luke 12:32)[11]

Don't be afraid; just believe.
(Mark 5:36)[12]

When I am afraid, I will trust in you.
(Psalm 56:3)[13]

Surely God is my salvation; I will trust and not be afraid.
(Isaiah 12:2)[14]

I sought the LORD, and he answered me; he delivered me from all my fears.
(Psalm 34:4)[15]

The Lord is near. Do not be anxious about anything.
(Philippians 4:5,6)[16]

Therefore we will not fear, though the earth give way and the mountains fall into the heart of the sea, though its waters roar and foam and the mountains quake with their surging.
(Psalm 46:2-3)[17]

what human beings can do to us as we walk on this earth.[18] The worst thing a human being can do is to take our life (they cannot touch our souls).[19] But God has infinitely more power; He can destroy your body and put your soul in hell.[20] Therefore, the only thing we should properly fear is God alone—who has the power to send our bodies and souls into hell for eternity. This type of fear is the beginning of knowledge and wisdom.[21]

Finally, as Christians, we should stand firm in our faith and never fear giving our testimony and spreading the gospel.[22] When we became Christians, God did not give us a spirit of fear, but a spirit of power, of love and of self-discipline.[23]

Fear of man will prove to be a snare, but whoever trusts in the LORD is kept safe.
(Proverbs 29:25)[18]

I tell you, my friends, do not be afraid of those who kill the body and after that can do no more. But I will show you whom you should fear: Fear him who, after the killing of the body, has the power to throw you into hell. Yes, I tell you, fear him.
(Luke 12:4-5)[19]

Do not be afraid of those who kill the body but cannot kill the soul. Rather, be afraid of the One who can destroy both soul and body in hell.
(Matthew 10:28)[20]

The fear of the LORD is the beginning of knowledge.
(Proverbs 1:7)[21]

Stand firm in one spirit, contending as one man for the faith of the gospel without being frightened in any way by those who oppose you.
(Philippians 1:27-28)[22]

For God did not give us a spirit of timidity, but a spirit of power, of love and of self-discipline.
(2 Timothy 1:7)[23]

To obtain a free audio recording entitled:

"Overcoming Anxiety,"

Please Visit: Counseling4Christians.com

Lesson 6

Backsliding

> "So, if you think you are standing firm,
> be careful you don't fall!"
> **(1 Corinthians 10:12)**

Backslide: to regress; to slip backwards or revert to a previous, worse state

Has your faith become dull and lacking in enthusiasm? Have you drifted out of the habit of reading the Bible, praying, attending church, helping others, and witnessing to those who do not know Christ? Are you lazy, undisciplined, and lacking in self-control? Are you trapped in life-dominating sins? Is your conscience seared to the point that you no longer experience godly sorrow when you sin?

"Backsliding" is a recurring theme throughout the Bible—God's people falling away from their faith and belief in Him and falling back into sin. The process can be slow and gradual, or sudden; unfortunately, the result is always the same. We fall away from our close personal relationship with God and fall into spiritual dullness or outright sin and disobedience.

God deplores our backsliding and desires that we return to our former relationship with Him. He personally appeals to us to return, and He disciplines those who do not.

If you feel that you are starting to backslide, stay alert and remain self-controlled. If you feel you are already in a state of spiritual dullness, or if you feel trapped in sinful behavior, turn your heart back to God and His love. He is waiting for you with open arms.

Please read on...

Synopsis

Most people are "on fire" for the Lord when they first become Christians—when they are "born again." However, slowly over time, their enthusiasm can begin to grow cold as they live out their lives in a fallen and sin-filled world.

Sometimes the process of backsliding is largely a "passive" process, whereby the believer gradually drifts away from a Spirit-filled relationship with God. The Bible uses a variety of terms to describe this process:

- Forgetting God[1]
- Heart Turning Away From God[2,3]
- Forsaking Your First Love[4]
- Turning Away From The Gospel[5]

If you ever forget the LORD your God and follow other gods and worship and bow down to them, I testify against you today that you will surely be destroyed.
(Deuteronomy 8:19)[1]

The LORD became angry with Solomon because his heart had turned away from the LORD, the God of Israel, who had appeared to him twice. Although he had forbidden Solomon to follow other gods, Solomon did not keep the LORD's command.
(1 Kings 11:9-10)[2]

This is what the LORD says: "Cursed is the one who trusts in man, who depends on flesh for his strength and whose heart turns away from the LORD.
(Jeremiah 17:5)[3]

Yet I hold this against you: You have forsaken your first love. Remember the height from which you have fallen! Repent, and do the things you did at first.
(Revelation 2:4-5)[4]

I am astonished that you are so quickly deserting the one who called you by the grace of Christ and are turning to a different gospel—which is really no gospel at all. Evidently some people are throwing you into confusion and are trying to pervert the gospel of Christ. **(Galatians 1:6-7)**[5]

- Wandering From The Faith[6,7]
- Becoming Lazy[8]
- Being Complacent[9]
- Being Lukewarm[10]

Other Scriptures suggest that backsliding can take the form of a more conscious and "active" role in the decision to turn to evil and disobey God. The end product of this decision can be slavery to sin.

- Turning To Follow Satan[11]
- Becoming Slaves To Sin[12]
- Being Taken Captive By Satan[13]
- Turning To Evil[14]

> They have left the straight way and wandered off to follow the way of Balaam son of Boer, who loved the wages of wickedness.
> **(2 Peter 2:15)**[6]

> Some people, eager for money, have wandered from the faith and pierced themselves with many griefs.
> **(1 Timothy 6:10)**[7]

> God is not unjust; he will not forget your work and the love you have shown him as you have helped his people and continue to help them. We want each of you to show this same diligence to the very end, in order to make your hope sure. We do not want you to become lazy, but to imitate those who through faith and patience inherit what has been promised.
> **(Hebrews 6:10-12)**[8]

> The complacency of fools will destroy them.
> **(Proverbs 1:32)**[9]

> *So, because you are lukewarm—neither hot nor cold—I am about to spit you out of my mouth.*
> **(Revelation 3:16)**[10]

> Some have in fact already turned away to follow Satan.
> **(1 Timothy 5:15)**[11]

> *They promise them freedom, while they themselves are slaves of depravity—for a man is a slave to whatever has mastered him.*
> **(2 Peter 2:19)**[12]

The Bible also describes the condition of "backsliding" metaphorically, as:

- Salt Losing It's Saltiness[15]
- Being Asleep[16]
- Serving Two Masters[17]
- Grass Without Water[18]
- Seed Sown Among Thorns[19]

Those who oppose him he must gently instruct, in the hope that God will grant them repentance leading them to a knowledge of the truth, and that they will come to their senses and escape from the trap of the devil, who has taken them captive to do his will.
(2 Timothy 2:25-26)[13]

Do good, O LORD, to those who are good, to those who are upright in heart. But those who turn to crooked ways the LORD will banish with the evildoers.
(Psalm 125:4-5)[14]

You are the salt of the earth. But if the salt loses its saltiness, how can it be made salty again? It is no longer good for anything, except to be thrown out and trampled by men.
(Matthew 5:13)[15]

So then, let us not be like others, who are asleep, but let us be alert and self-controlled.
(1 Thessalonians 5:6)[16]

No servant can serve two masters. Either he will hate the one and love the other, or he will be devoted to the one and despise the other. You cannot serve both God and Money.
(Luke 16:13)[17]

Can papyrus grow tall where there is no marsh? Can reeds thrive without water? While still growing and uncut, they wither more quickly than grass. Such is the destiny of all who forget God; so perishes the hope of the godless.
(Job 8:11-13)[18]

Still others, like seed sown among thorns, hear the word; but the worries of this life, the deceitfulness of wealth and the desires for other things come in and choke the word, making it unfruitful.
(Mark 4:18-19)[19]

- A Dead Branch[20]
- Building A House Without A Firm Foundation[21]
- Being Taken Captive Through Hollow And Deceptive Philosophy[22]

All Christians backslide temporarily at one point or another in their lives; however, remaining in a state of indifference, or sinful separation from God, can have serious outcomes. As time progresses, our hearts may become hardened through backsliding[23] and our consciences may become "seared."[24]

That's one reason why God recommends that we examine ourselves to see if we are living fully in the faith.[25] We can undertake this

---

If anyone does not remain in me, he is like a branch that is thrown away and withers; such branches are picked up, thrown into the fire and burned.
(John 15:6)[20]

But everyone who hears these words of mine and does not put them into practice is like a foolish man who built his house on sand. The rain came down, the streams rose, and the winds blew and beat against that house, and it fell with a great crash.
(Matthew 7:26-27)[21]

See to it that no one takes you captive through hollow and deceptive philosophy, which depends on human tradition and the basic principles of this world rather than on Christ.
(Colossians 2:8)[22]

You will be ever hearing but never understanding; you will be ever seeing but never perceiving. For this people's heart has become calloused; they hardly hear with their ears, and they have closed their eyes.
(Matthew 13:14-15)[23]

Such teachings come from hypocritical liars, whose consciences have been seared with a hot iron.
(1 Timothy 4:2)[24]

Examine yourselves to see whether you are in the faith; test yourselves. Do you not realize that Christ Jesus is in you—unless, of course, you fail the test.
(2 Corinthians 13:5)[25]

self-evaluation by looking at the fruit that our lives are bearing.[26] Are we reaching others for Christ? Are we helping to change lives? If not, then we are almost certainly backsliding.

In the end, backsliding always has negative and bitter consequences.[27] God wants us to return to Him.[28] He wants us to be alert and self-controlled.[29] He wants us to repent[30] and do the things we did when we first knew Him.[31]

Because God loves us so much, He disciplines His children when they drift away from Him or fall back into sin.[32,33] Everyone who sins is disciplined. If you are not disciplined, then you are not true children of God.[34] No discipline seems pleasant at the time we re-

---

This is to my Father's glory, that you bear much fruit, showing yourselves to be my disciples.
(John 15:8)[26]

"Your wickedness will punish you; your backsliding will rebuke you. Consider then and realize how evil and bitter it is for you when you forsake the Lord your God and have no awe of me," declares the Lord, the Lord Almighty.
(Jeremiah 2:19)[27]

"Return, faithless people; I will cure you of backsliding."
"Yes, we will come to you, for you are the Lord our God."
(Jeremiah 3:22)[28]

So then, let us not be like others, who are asleep, but let us be alert and self-controlled.
(1 Thessalonians 5:6)[29]

He is patient with you, not wanting anyone to perish, but everyone to come to repentance.
(2 Peter 3:9)[30]

Repent, and do the things you did at first.
(Revelation 2:5)[31]

You rebuke and discipline men for their sin.
(Psalm 39:11)[32]

Blessed is the man whom God corrects; so do not despise the discipline of the Almighty. For he wounds, but he also binds up; he injures, but his hands also heal.
(Job 5:17-18)[33]

ceive it, but later on it produces a "harvest of righteousness and peace" for those who are trained by it.[35] Bottom line, consider yourself blessed if you are being disciplined for your backsliding.[36]

Be prepared![37] Our time on earth is short and Christ will be returning soon. We need to have our lives in order when He comes, for He will come "like a thief in the night—at a time when we do not expect Him.[38,39] We need to wake up from our slumber and turn back to God, for He is coming soon.[40,41]

> If you are not disciplined (and everyone undergoes discipline),
> then you are illegitimate children and not true sons.
> **(Hebrews 12:8)**[34]
>
> No discipline seems pleasant at the time, but painful. Later
> on, however, it produces a harvest of righteousness
> and peace for those who have been trained by it.
> **(Hebrews 12:11)**[35]
>
> Blessed is the man you discipline, O LORD,
> the man you teach from your law.
> **(Psalm 94:12)**[36]
>
> Do your best to present yourself to God as one approved,
> a workman who does not need to be ashamed and
> who correctly handles the word of truth.
> **(2 Timothy 2:15)**[37]
>
> The day of the Lord will come
> like a thief in the night.
> **(1 Thessalonians 5:2)**[38]
>
> *You must be ready, because the Son of Man will come*
> *at an hour when you do not expect him.*
> **(Luke 12:40)**[39]
>
> The hour has come for you to wake up from your slumber,
> because our salvation is nearer now than
> when we first believed.
> **(Romans 13:11)**[40]
>
> *Behold, I am coming soon!*
> **(Revelation 22:7)**[41]

God's Guidance

Human beings are weak but God is strong.[42] He stands knocking at the door, and wants us to return to Him.[43] Through the power of God, we have been given everything we need to live a life of godliness,[44] and to escape backsliding and the corruption of the world that is caused by evil desires.[45] The Lord knows how to rescue godly men from trials.[46] Repent! And turn back to God.[47] Come back to your senses and stop sinning.[48]

If you think you are standing firm in your faith, be careful you don't fall.[49] If you don't stand firm in your faith, you won't stand at

---

> Look to the LORD and his strength; seek his face always.
> **(Psalm 105:4)**[42]

> *Here I am! I stand at the door and knock. If anyone hears my voice and opens the door, I will come in and eat with him, and he with me.*
> **(Revelation 3:20)**[43]

> His divine power has given us everything we need for life and godliness through our knowledge of him who called us by his own glory and goodness.
> **(2 Peter 1:3)**[44]

> Through these he has given us his very great and precious promises, so that through them you may participate in the divine nature and escape the corruption in the world caused by evil desires.
> **(2 Peter 1:4)**[45]

> The Lord knows how to rescue godly men from trials and to hold the unrighteous for the day of judgment.
> **(2 Peter 2:9)**[46]

> Let him turn to the LORD, and he will have mercy on him, and to our God, for he will freely pardon.
> **(Isaiah 55:7)**[47]

> Come back to your senses as you ought, and stop sinning.
> **(1 Corinthians 15:34)**[48]

> So, if you think you are standing firm, be careful you don't fall!
> **(1 Corinthians 10:12)**[49]

all.[50] Let nothing move you; always give yourself fully to the Lord.[51] Hold on to the confidence and enthusiasm you had when you first knew God.[52]

Don't swerve to the left or to the right; keep your feet from evil.[53] Sow righteousness.[54] Keep growing spiritually. Make every effort to add to your faith: goodness; knowledge; self-control; perseverance; godliness; brotherly kindness; and love.[55] Aim for perfection; don't settle for "good enough."[56] God doesn't like lukewarm Christians.[57]

Resist the devil and he will flee from you.[58] Just as Satan tempted

---

If you do not stand firm in your faith, you will not stand at all.
(Isaiah 7:9)[50]

Therefore, my dear brothers, stand firm. Let nothing move you. Always give yourselves fully to the work of the Lord, because you know that your labor in the Lord is not in vain.
(1 Corinthians 15:58)[51]

We have come to share in Christ if we hold firmly till the end the confidence we had at first.
(Hebrews 3:14)[52]

Do not swerve to the right or the left; keep your foot from evil.
(Proverbs 4:27)[53]

Sow for yourselves righteousness, reap the fruit of unfailing love, and break up your unplowed ground; for it is time to seek the LORD, until he comes and showers righteousness on you.
(Hosea 10:12)[54]

For this very reason, make every effort to add to your faith goodness; and to goodness, knowledge; and to knowledge, self-control; and to self-control, perseverance; and to perseverance, godliness; and to godliness, brotherly kindness; and to brotherly kindness, love. **(2 Peter 1:5-7)**[55]

Aim for perfection. **(2 Corinthians 13:11)**[56]

I know your deeds. You are neither hot nor cold. Because you are lukewarm—neither hot nor cold—I am about to spit you out of my mouth. **(Revelation 3:15-16)**[57]

Resist the devil, and he will flee from you.
(James 4:7)[58]

Jesus when He was weak,[59] he will tempt us when we have our guard down and are distracted by the world.[60] Pray to God for strength and protection from the evil one.[61] In fact, devote yourself to prayer, being watchful that you do not backslide, and thankful that you know our Lord and Savior, Jesus Christ.[62]

Read the Bible on a regular basis, and study the Scriptures.[63] Do not neglect God's Word.[64] Hide the Word of God in your heart, so that you don't slip away from Him and fall into sin.[65]

In the end, make every effort to live holy and godly lives.[66] Conduct yourselves in a manner worthy of the gospel of Christ.[67]

> Then Jesus was led by the Spirit into the desert to be tempted by the devil. After fasting forty days and forty nights, he was hungry. The tempter came to him and said, "If you are the Son of God, tell these stones to become bread."
> **(Matthew 4:1-3)**[59]

> *Watch and pray so that you will not fall into temptation. The spirit is willing, but the body is weak.*
> **(Matthew 26:41)**[60]

> But the Lord is faithful, and he will strengthen and protect you from the evil one.
> **(2 Thessalonians 3:3)**[61]

> Devote yourselves to prayer, being watchful and thankful.
> **(Colossians 4:2)**[62]

> When your words came, I ate them; they were my joy and my heart's delight, for I bear your name, O LORD God Almighty.
> **(Jeremiah 15:16)**[63]

> I will not neglect your word.
> **(Psalm 119:16)**[64]

> I have hidden your word in my heart that I might not sin against you.
> **(Psalm 119:11)**[65]

> Since everything will be destroyed in this way, what kind of people ought you to be? You ought to live holy and godly lives as you look forward to the day of God and speed its coming.
> **(2 Peter 3:11)**[66]

> Whatever happens, conduct yourselves in a manner worthy of the gospel of Christ. **(Philippians 1:27)**[67]

Lesson 7

Belief/Salvation

*"For God so loved the world that he gave his one
and only Son, that whoever believes in him
shall not perish but have eternal life."*
(John 3:16)

Belief: the acceptance or conviction that certain
things (or claims) are true or real

What you believe has a profound influence on your entire existence. If you believe in Jesus Christ, when you die you will go to heaven and live forever in paradise with God. If you do not believe in Him, when you die you will go to hell where you will be separated from God and suffer for eternity. Given this alternative, it is staggering that more people do not thoroughly evaluate the evidence for the life, death, and resurrection of Jesus Christ, as told in the Holy Bible.

Synopsis

The story of Jesus Christ begins at the point of creation. Jesus was with God (and the Holy Spirit) when the world and everything in it was created—including mankind.[1,2] When God saw the world and all that He had made, He said that it was "good."[3] Unfortunately, it did not stay that way for long.

In the beginning was the Word [Jesus], and the Word
was with God, and the Word was God.
(John 1:1)[1]

He was with God in the beginning.
(John 1:2)[2]

God saw all that he had made,
and it was very good.
(Genesis 1:31)[3]

Adam and Eve, the first man and woman, disobeyed God in the Garden of Eden, when they "gave in" to Satan's temptation[4,5] and ate the fruit that God had forbidden them to eat.[6] At that point, sin entered into the world. As a result, all human beings inherit a sinful nature and all human beings suffer a physical death.[7]

God cannot tolerate sin.[8] Therefore, the fall of mankind into sin separated us from the all-loving God who created us. Because of this separation, our Heavenly Father, in His great mercy, decided to send His one and only Son, Jesus Christ[9,10] to take away the sins of the world[11,12] so that our relationship with Him could be restored.[13,14]

> Now the serpent [Satan] was more crafty than any of the wild animals the LORD God had made. He said to the woman, "Did God really say, 'You must not eat from any tree in the garden'?"
> **(Genesis 3:1)**[4]

> "You will not surely die," the serpent said to the woman. For God knows that when you eat of it your eyes will be opened, and you will be like God, knowing good and evil.
> **(Genesis 3:4)**[5]

> When the woman [Eve] saw that the fruit of the tree was good for food and pleasing to the eye, and also desirable for gaining wisdom, she took some and ate it. She also gave some to her husband [Adam], who was with her, and he ate it.
> **(Genesis 3:6)**[6]

> For as in Adam all die, so in Christ all will be made alive.
> **(1 Corinthians 15:22)**[7]

> But your iniquities have separated you from your God;
> your sins have hidden his face from you,
> so that he will not hear.
> **(Isaiah 59:2)**[8]

> *I have not come on my own; but he sent me.*
> **(John 8:42)**[9]

> This is love: not that we loved God, but that he loved us and sent his Son as an atoning sacrifice for our sins.
> **(1 John 4:10)**[10]

> He appeared so that he might take away our sins.
> **(1 John 3:5)**[11]

Jesus entered this world as a human baby.[15] Through the power of the Holy Spirit, a young woman named Mary, a virgin, miraculously became pregnant with Jesus,[16] and later gave birth to Him in the city of Bethlehem. When He was born, an angel of the Lord told Mary to name her new baby "Jesus," [which literally means, "Jehovah saves"], "because He will save His people from their sins." (Matthew 1:21)

As Jesus grew up, He shared in our human experience. He was all-God,[17] yet all-human. He was tempted in every way that man is tempted,[18] and He felt pain and human emotions.[19] However, unlike man, Jesus was perfect, and did not sin.[20]

> Look, the Lamb of God who takes away the sin of the world!
> **(John 1:29)**[12]

> But we also rejoice in God through our Lord Jesus Christ, through whom we have now received reconciliation.
> **(Romans 5:11)**[13]

> In him [Christ] and through faith in him we may approach God with freedom and confidence.
> **(Ephesians 3:12)**[14]

> The Word [Jesus] became flesh and made his dwelling among us.
> **(John 1:14)**[15]

> She [Mary] was found to be with child through the Holy Spirit.
> **(Matthew 1:18)**[16]

> *I and the Father are one.*
> **(John 10:30)**[17]

> Because he himself suffered when he was tempted, he is able to help those who are being tempted.
> **(Hebrews 2:18)**[18]

> During the days of Jesus' life on earth, he offered up prayers and petitions with loud cries and tears to the one who could save him from death, and he was heard because of his reverent submission.
> **(Hebrews 5:7)**[19]

> For we do not have a high priest who is unable to sympathize with our weaknesses, but we have one who has been tempted in every way, just as we are—yet was without sin.
> **(Hebrews 4:15)**[20]

Throughout His ministry on earth, Jesus told people about God and why He was sent to this earth.[21,22] He urged people to repent of their sins, and turn from their evil ways.[23] He made it very clear that the only way human beings could restore their relationship with God was through belief in Him, and in Him only.[24,25]

Jesus preached that if people would believe in Him, they would be "born again."[26] He urged them to be baptized as an outward expression of their spiritual cleansing and "rebirth."[27] He made it clear that the process of being "born again" is essential to salvation.[26] When we accept Jesus Christ as our Lord and Savior, we are a new creation, and life is never the same again.[28]

I have come into the world as a light, so that no one who believes in me should stay in darkness.
(John 12:46)[21]

I have come so that they may have life, and have it to the full.
(John 10:10)[22]

The kingdom of God is near. Repent and believe the good news!
(Mark 1:15)[23]

I am the way and the truth and the life. No one comes to the Father except through me.
(John 14:6)[24]

I am the gate; whoever enters through me will be saved.
(John 10:9)[25]

I tell you the truth, no one can see the kingdom of God unless he is born again.
(John 3:3)[26]

I tell you the truth, no one can enter the kingdom unless he is born of water and the Spirit.
(John 3:5)[27]

Therefore, if anyone is in Christ, he is a new creation; the old has gone, the new has come!
(2 Corinthians 5:17)[28]

Belief/Salvation 57

During His time on earth, Jesus performed many miracles in the hope that people would see His power, and realize that He was not just any ordinary man—but that He was divine.[29] Unfortunately, many people did not recognize His divine nature or believe in Him, even after the awesome miracles he performed.[30,31] Even His own brothers did not believe in Him.[32]

As time passed, people began to hate Jesus for no reason[33] and plotted to kill Him. They looked for evidence against Him,[34] even though He was entirely innocent and sinless[35] and did nothing to deserve such treatment.[33]

Jesus was arrested, tried and convicted of heresy, and sentenced to death by crucifixion. He endured incredible suffering. He was stripped and flogged.[36] They spit on Him and struck Him on the

---

Do not believe me unless I do what my Father does. But if I do it, even though you do not believe me, believe the miracles, that you may know and understand that the Father is in me, and I in the Father.
(John 10:37-38)[29]

He was in the world, and though the world was made through him, the world did not recognize him.
(John 1:10)[30]

Even after Jesus had done all these miraculous signs in their presence, they still would not believe in him.
(John 12:37)[31]

For even his own brothers did not believe in him.
(John 7:5)[32]

But now they have seen these miracles, and yet they have hated both me and my Father. But this is to fulfill what is written in their Law: *"They hated me without reason."*
(John 15:24-25)[33]

The chief priests and the whole Sanhedrin were looking for false evidence against Jesus so that they could put him to death.
(Matthew 26:59)[34]

God made him who had no sin to be sin for us.
(2 Corinthians 5:21)[35]

Then Pilate took Jesus and had him flogged.
(John 19:1)[36]

head repeatedly.[37] They mocked Him and crucified Him.[38] He died an excruciatingly painful death[39,40] and was buried in a tomb.[41]

On the third day after His death, the followers of Jesus went to His tomb and found that it was empty. Jesus had miraculously risen from the dead.[42] He appeared to His disciples in His "glorified body" and proved to them, on a number of occasions, that He was not dead, but alive.[43] On the 40th day after His death, Jesus ascended into heaven to sit at the right hand of God the Father Almighty.[44]

> They spit on him, and took the staff and struck him on the head again and again.
> **(Matthew 27:30)**[37]

> After they had mocked him, they took off the robe and put his own clothes on him. Then they led him away to crucify him.
> **(Matthew 27:31)**[38]

> And when Jesus had cried out again in a loud voice, he gave up his spirit.
> **(Matthew 27:50)**[39]

> But when they [the Roman soldiers] came to Jesus and found that he was already dead, they did not break his legs. Instead, one of the soldiers pierced Jesus' side with a spear, bringing a sudden flow of blood and water.
> **(John 19:33-34)**[40]

> As evening approached, there came a rich man from Arimathea, named Joseph, who had himself become a disciple of Jesus. Going to Pilate, he asked for Jesus' body, and Pilate ordered that it be given to him. Joseph took the body, wrapped it in a clean linen cloth, and placed it in his own new tomb that he had cut out of the rock. He rolled a big stone in front of the entrance of the tomb and went away.
> **(Matthew 27:57-60)**[41]

> The angel said to the women, "Do not be afraid, for I know that you are looking for Jesus, who was crucified. He is not here; he has risen, just as he said."
> **(Matthew 28:5-6)**[42]

> After his suffering, he showed himself to these men and gave many convincing proofs that he was alive. He appeared to them over a period of forty days and spoke about the kingdom of God.
> **(Acts 1:3)**[43]

Belief/Salvation

The disciples of Jesus were first-hand witnesses to His life, death, and resurrection.[45] They were certain of what they saw and heard, and they went on to preach the "good news" of the gospel of Jesus Christ throughout the nations of the world.[46]

The good news is this: while we were still sinners, Christ died for us.[47] Anyone who believes in Him, will receive forgiveness of sins,[48] will be reconciled with God,[49] and will live forever in heaven.[50]

When Jesus went to be with the Father, He did not leave us alone. He promised that He would send the Holy Spirit, the great Counselor, who would live and dwell within the hearts of all believers.[51]

While he was blessing them, he left them
and was taken up into heaven.
(Luke 24:51)[44]

The man [the apostle John] who saw it [the crucifixion] has given testimony, and his testimony is true. He knows that he tells the truth, and he testifies so that you also may believe.
(John 19:35)[45]

We did not follow cleverly invented stories when we told you about the power and coming of our Lord Jesus Christ, but we were eyewitnesses of his majesty.
(2 Peter 1:16)[46]

But God demonstrates his own love for us in this: while we were still sinners, Christ died for us.
(Romans 5:8)[47]

Everyone who believes in him receives forgiveness of sins through his name.
(Acts 10:43)[48]

God was reconciling the world to himself in Christ, not counting men's sins against them.
(2 Corinthians 5:19)[49]

I tell you the truth, he who believes has everlasting life. **(John 6:47)**[50]

And I will ask the Father, and he will give you another Counselor to be with you forever—the Spirit of truth. **(John 14:16-17)**[51]

Belief/Salvation

The Holy Spirit guides us into all truth[50] and testifies with our spirit that we are God's children.[51]

At some point in the future (at a time unknown to man) Jesus Christ will again return to earth (the "second coming of Christ") to bring salvation for those who are saved and who are waiting for His return.[52] Importantly, when He returns He will pass a final judgment on all mankind—those who are still living, and those who have died.[53] This fact is of utmost importance!

When Jesus returns again, if you have not yet received Him into your heart and believe that He died for your sins, you will be condemned to hell for eternity.[54] On the other hand, if you confess with your mouth, "Jesus is Lord," and believe in your heart that God raised Him from the dead, you will be saved."[55]

But when he, the Spirit of truth, comes, he will guide you into all truth.
(James 16:13)[50]

The Spirit himself testifies with our spirit that we are God's children.
(Romans 8:16)[51]

And he [Jesus] will appear a second time, not to bear sin, but to bring salvation to those who are waiting for him.
(Hebrews 9:27-28)[52]

For we must all appear before the judgment seat of Christ, that each one may receive what is due him for the things done while in the body, whether good or bad.
(2 Corinthians 5:10)[53]

They will be punished with everlasting destruction and shut out from the presence of the Lord and from the majesty of his power on the day he comes to be glorified in his holy people and to be marveled at among all those who have believed.
(2 Thessalonians 1:9-10)[54]

If you confess with your mouth, "Jesus is Lord," and believe in your heart that God raised him from the dead, you will be saved.
(Romans 10:9)[55]

Importantly, God desires that *all* men be saved and come to a knowledge of truth.[56,57] That includes you, and everyone on this planet. Whoever believes in Jesus Christ and the one who sent Him, crosses over from death into eternal life.[58]

Conclusion

There are no magic words that you can say that will get you into heaven, and save you from hell. Only a sincere belief that Christ is Lord, the Son of the Living God, and that He died on the cross for your sins, and was raised from the dead by God, will secure eternal salvation and life everlasting. If you sincerely believe these things, the following prayer is offered to help express what has already taken place in your heart.

The "Sinner's Prayer"

I confess that I am a sinner. I sincerely repent of all my wrongdoings. I believe that you sent Jesus Christ, your one and only Son, to die for my sins on the cross at Calvary. I believe that Jesus is Lord, and that you raised Him from the dead after His crucifixion. I believe that He sits at your right hand in heaven, and that when I die, I will see Jesus "face-to-face," and dwell in your house forever.

A Final Word...

If this is the first time that you have accepted Jesus Christ as your Lord and Savior, it is important to understand that you may come under increasing attack by the Evil One (the Devil). Pray to God for strength to resist Satan, and surround yourself with other believers. Pray regularly, and keep reading the Bible.

God our Savior...wants all men to be saved and to come to a knowledge of the truth. **(1 Timothy 2:3-4)**[56]

For my Father's will is that everyone who looks to the Son and believes in him shall have eternal life, and I will raise him up at the last day. **(John 6:40)**[57]

I tell you the truth, whoever hears my word and believes him who sent me has eternal life and will not be condemned; he has crossed over from death to life. **(John 5:24)**[58]

Lesson 8

Christ, Who He Is

Some people have never heard of Jesus Christ. Others believe that he was a prophet, but not God—and that He never claimed to be God. Let's listen to Jesus in His own words as He tells us who He is. These are either the outrageous claims of someone who is mentally ill, or these are the claims of the God of the universe. You must decide.

I am the First and the Last.
(Revelation 1:17)

⌘

"I am the Alpha and the Omega," says the Lord God,
*"who is, and who was, and who
is to come, the Almighty."*
(Revelation 1:8)

⌘

*Before Abraham was born,
I am!*
(John 8:58)

⌘

I and the Father are one.
(John 10:30)

I am God's Son.
(John 10:36)

⌘

*I am in my Father, and you are in me,
and I am in you.*
(John 14:20)

⌘

I am from him and he sent me.
(John 7:29)

⌘

For I came from God and now am here.
(John 8:42)

⌘

*I am the Root and the Offspring of David,
and the bright Morning Star.*
(Revelation 22:16)

⌘

*I am the light of the world. Whoever follows me
will never walk in darkness,
but will have the light of life.*
(John 8:12)

⌘

*I am the bread of life.
He who comes to me will never go hungry,
and he who believes in me
will never be thirsty.*
(John 6:35)

*I am the living bread that came down from heaven.
If anyone eats of this bread, he will live forever.*
(John 6:51)

⌘

*I am the good shepherd.
The good shepherd
lays down his life
for the sheep.*
(John 10:11)

⌘

*I am the gate;
whoever enters through me
will be saved.*
(John 10:9)

⌘

*I am the way and the truth and the life.
No one comes to the Father
except through me.*
(John 14:6)

⌘

I am among you as one who serves.
(Luke 22:27)

I am not here on my own, but he who sent me is true.
You do not know him, but I know him because
I am from him and he sent me.
(John 7:28-29)

⌘

You are from below; I am from above.
You are of this world;
I am not of this world.
(John 8:23)

⌘

I am the Living One; I was dead,
and behold I am alive
for ever and ever!
And I hold the keys
of death and Hades.
(Revelation 1:18)

⌘

I am the resurrection and the life.
He who believes in me will live,
even though he dies;
and whoever lives and believes in me
will never die.
(John 11:25-26)

Lesson 9

Citizenship

"The authorities that exist have been
established by God."
(Romans 13:1)

Citizen: a person who is legally recognized as
a member of a city, state, or country

We live in a world of political unrest. As Christians, it is sometimes difficult to determine what type of relationship we should have to our government and to the laws of the land. Fortunately, God's Word contains important advice on the topic of citizenship. It also addresses the topic of civil disobedience.

Synopsis

First of all, we should remember that God alone is the ultimate authority for our lives and our actions.[1,2] We must seek to follow His commands.[3,4] Any man-made authority (government) is subject to

---

Fear the LORD your God, serve him only and
take your oaths in his name.
(Deuteronomy 6:13)[1]

All your words are true; all your righteous laws are eternal.
(Psalm 119:160)[2]

I have chosen the way of truth; I have set my heart on your laws.
(Psalm 119:30)[3]

Teach me, O LORD, to follow your decrees;
then I will keep them to the end.
(Psalm 119:33)[4]

There is no authority except that which God has established.
The authorities that exist have been established by God.
(Romans 13:1)[5]

God's authority.[5] We are citizens of heaven first, and then citizens of this world.[6]

As a general rule, God wants us to obey our leaders and submit to their authority.[7,8] The authorities that exist have been established by God.[5] If you rebel against authority, you are rebelling against what God has instituted and, if you do so, you will bring judgment upon yourself.[9]

In most instances, if you do what is right and follow the law, there is no reason to fear the government or authorities.[10] Police officers and other authorities are intended to be servants who help and do good.[11]

Authorities also exist in order to punish wrongdoers.[11] We are to obey authorities, not only because of possible punishment, but

---

But our citizenship is in heaven. And we eagerly await
a Savior from there, the Lord Jesus Christ.
(Philippians 3:20)[6]

Obey your leaders and submit to their authority.
(Hebrews 13:17)[7]

Submit yourselves for the Lord's sake to every
authority instituted among men.
(1 Peter 2:13)[8]

He who rebels against the authority is rebelling against
what God has instituted, and those who do so will
bring judgment on themselves.
(Romans 13:2)[9]

For rulers hold no terror for those who do right, but for
those who do wrong. Do you want to be free from fear
of the one in authority? Then do what is right and
he will commend you.
(Romans 13:3)[10]

For he is God's servant to do you good. But if you do wrong,
be afraid, for he does not bear the sword for nothing.
He is God's servant, an agent of wrath to bring
punishment on the wrongdoer.
(Romans 13:4)[11]

also because our conscience tells us it is the right thing to do.[12] This is also why we should pay taxes—because it is the right thing to do.[13,14]

Jesus Himself reminded people to pay their taxes, and He was careful to pay His own.[15] On one occasion, He even performed a miracle in order to make sure His taxes, and those of His disciples, were paid.[16]

Under ordinary circumstances, God's overall desire is for us to be subject to rulers and authorities, to do good, and to live peacefully and humbly with all men.[17] However, when God's law runs contrary to man's law, then some forms of civil disobedience may be acceptable, or even necessary.

Therefore, it is necessary to submit to authorities, not only because of possible punishment but also because of conscience.
(Romans 13:5)[12]

This is why you pay taxes, for the authorities are God's servants, who give their full time to governing.
(Romans 13:6)[13]

Give everyone what you owe him: If you owe taxes, pay taxes; if revenue, then revenue; if respect, then respect; if honor, then honor.
(Romans 13:7)[14]

Give to Caesar what is Caesar's and to God what is God's.
(Mark 12:17)[15]

But so that we may not offend them, go to the lake and throw out your line. Take the first fish you catch; open its mouth and you will find a four-drachma coin. Take it and give it to them for my tax and yours.
(Matthew 17:27)[16]

Remind the people to be subject to rulers and authorities, to be obedient, to be ready to do whatever is good, to slander no one, to be peaceable and considerate, and to show true humility toward all men.
(Titus 3:1-2)[17]

For example, when the apostles were given a direct command by authorities not to preach in Jesus' name, under threat of going to jail, Peter and the other apostles with him stated: "We must obey God rather than men."[18]

We know that at least some of the original apostles later on became martyrs and paid with their lives because they obeyed God's command (to spread the gospel) rather than man's commands.[19]

Note: There are many lawful and peaceful forms of Christian action that can be taken within a democratic society to bring about changes in man's laws. Voting, petitions, peaceful demonstrations, and lawful protests, would all be acceptable (and legal) methods of bringing about change.

Peter and the other apostles replied:
"We must obey God rather than men!"
(Acts 5:29)[18]

It was about this time that King Herod arrested some who belonged to the church, intending to persecute them. He had James, the brother of John, put to death with the sword. When he saw that this pleased the Jews, he proceeded to seize Peter also.
(Acts 12:1-3)[19]

Lesson 10

Communication

"The tongue has the power of life and death."
(Proverbs 18:21)

Lying: to make an untrue statement or give false information
Deceit: the act or attempt to trick or mislead
Slander: a false, malicious statement which injures reputation
Gossip: rumor or idle talk about someone
Quarrel: a verbal dispute or heated argument

As Christians, the way we communicate with others is extremely important. Our words can injure others, or they can heal. They can condemn, or they can be uplifting. They can be true and righteous, or they can be deceptive and false. The words we speak are a reflection of the condition of our faith and our walk with the Lord.

The Bible is overflowing with advice on how to communicate effectively with others, and how to avoid hurting others with careless speech.

Synopsis

Our words, whether good or bad, flow out of the condition of our heart.[1] That is, our words are indicators of our spiritual maturity.[2] Ideally, everything we say should be spoken with the utmost care

---

The good man brings good things out of the good stored up in his heart, and the evil man brings evil things out of the evil stored up in his heart. For out of the overflow of his heart his mouth speaks.
(Luke 6:45)[1]

If anyone considers himself religious and yet does not keep a tight rein on his tongue, he deceives himself and his religion is worthless.
(James 1:26)[2]

If anyone speaks, he should do it as one speaking the very words of God. **(1 Peter 4:11)**[3]

and consideration—"as if speaking the very words of God."[3] After all, the words we say can have tremendous influence on the lives of others, even to the point of influencing life and death.[4] Choose your words carefully, because on the day of judgment each of us will have to give an account for every careless word we have spoken.[5]

How to Speak:

<u>Be gentle and don't shout</u>.[6] Raising your voice and being harsh with another person tends to "stir up anger" and break down communication. People are much more likely to listen to you if you speak in a quiet voice.[7] Also, you'll be much more persuasive if you are patient and speak with a "gentle tongue" rather than shouting.[8]

<u>Control your anger</u>. Show restraint, and don't let yourself get out of control.[9,10] A hot-tempered man stirs up arguments and

---

The tongue has the power of life and death.
(Proverbs 18:21)[4]

But I tell you that men will have to give account on the day of judgment for every careless word they have spoken. For by your words you will be acquitted, and by your words you will be condemned.
(Matthew 12:36-37)[5]

A gentle answer turns away wrath, but a
harsh word stirs up anger.
(Proverbs 15:1)[6]

The quiet words of the wise are more to be heeded
than the shouts of a ruler of fools.
(Ecclesiastes 9:17)[7]

Through patience a ruler can be persuaded,
and a gentle tongue can break a bone.
(Proverbs 25:15)[8]

A fool gives full vent to his anger, but a wise man
keeps himself under control.
(Proverbs 29:11)[9]

Do not be quickly provoked in your spirit,
for anger resides in the lap of fools.
(Ecclesiastes 7:9)[10]

quarrels,[11,12] and is likely to commit many sins as a result of his anger.[13] If you are wise, you will try to remain even-tempered and show restraint when you speak to others.[14]

When to Speak:

<u>Think before you speak</u>.[15,16] Put a guard over your mouth and be careful what you say.[17,18] Don't speak too quickly.[19] Sometimes it is much better to "hold your tongue" and listen to the other

> A hot-tempered man stirs up dissension, but a patient man calms a quarrel.
> **(Proverbs 15:18)**[11]
>
> For as churning the milk produces butter, and as twisting the nose produces blood, so stirring up anger produces strife.
> **(Proverbs 30:33)**[12]
>
> An angry man stirs up dissension, and a hot-tempered one commits many sins.
> **(Proverbs 29:22)**[13]
>
> A man of knowledge uses words with restraint, and a man of understanding is even-tempered.
> **(Proverbs 17:27)**[14]
>
> He who guards his lips guards his life, but he who speaks rashly will come to ruin.
> **(Proverbs 13:3)**[15]
>
> The heart of the righteous weighs its answers, but the mouth of the wicked gushes evil.
> **(Proverbs 15:28)**[16]
>
> He who guards his mouth and his tongue keeps himself from calamity.
> **(Proverbs 21:23)**[17]
>
> Set a guard over my mouth, O LORD; keep watch over the door of my lips.
> **(Psalm 141:3)**[18]
>
> Do you see a man who speaks in haste? There is more hope for a fool than for him.
> **(Proverbs 29:20)**[19]

person before you answer.[20,21] You don't have to respond to everything another person says.[21] When you can see that a topic of conversation is going to lead to an argument, learn to drop the matter before a dispute breaks out.[23] Also, be patient and keep things in perspective; it is often wise to overlook an offense.[24]

<u>Avoid arguments and quarrels</u>. If you love to quarrel, you probably love to sin.[25] It is exceedingly difficult to live with a quarrelsome husband[26] or wife.[27-29] If at all possible, try to avoid strife

---

He who answers before listening—that is
his folly and his shame.
(Proverbs 18:13)[20]

When words are many, sin is not absent,
but he who holds his tongue is wise.
(Proverbs 10:19)[21]

Do not pay attention to every word people say.
(Ecclesiastes 7:21)[22]

Starting a quarrel is like breaching a dam;
so drop the matter before a dispute breaks out.
(Proverbs 17:14)[23]

A man's wisdom gives him patience;
it is to his glory to overlook an offense.
(Proverbs 19:11)[24]

He who loves a quarrel loves sin.
(Proverbs 17:19)[25]

As charcoal to embers and as wood to fire,
so is a quarrelsome man for kindling strife.
(Proverbs 26:21)[26]

A quarrelsome wife is like a constant dripping.
(Proverbs 19:13)[27]

Better to live in a desert than with a
quarrelsome and ill-tempered wife.
(Proverbs 21:19)[28]

A quarrelsome wife is like a constant dripping on a
rainy day; restraining her is like restraining the
wind or grasping oil with the hand.
(Proverbs 27:15-16)[29]

in your home.[30,31] Stand back and keep things in perspective; don't have anything to do with foolish or stupid arguments.[32] The Lord's servant must not quarrel.[33]

What Not to Say:

<u>Don't Stoop To The Other Person's Level</u>: If the conversation begins to deteriorate and the other person is being foolish or childish, be mature and don't stoop to his or her level.[34,35]

<u>Don't Mock Others</u>: Don't mock or make fun of others[36,37]

It is to a man's honor to avoid strife.
(Proverbs 20:3)[30]

Better a dry crust with peace and quiet than a house
full of feasting, with strife.
(Proverbs 17:1)[31]

Don't have anything to do with foolish and stupid arguments,
because you know they produce quarrels.
(2 Timothy 2:23)[32]

And the Lord's servant must not quarrel; instead,
he must be kind to everyone,
able to teach, not resentful.
(2 Timothy 2:24)[33]

Do not answer a fool according to his folly,
or you will be like him yourself.
(Proverbs 26:4)[34]

When I was a child, I talked like a child, I thought like a child,
I reasoned like a child. When I became a man,
I put childish ways behind me.
(1 Corinthians 13:11)[35]

Drive out the mocker, and out goes strife;
quarrels and insults are ended.
(Proverbs 22:10)[36]

*Again, anyone who says to his brother, "Raca" [worthless]
is answerable to the Sanhedrin. But anyone who says,
"You fool!" will be in danger of the fire of hell.*
(Matthew 5:22)[37]

or God may mock you; remain humble.[38] People who mock others resent being corrected.[39] No one likes a mocker.[40]

Don't Insult Others: If someone insults you, don't return the insult.[41] Just because you get insulted, you don't need to "insult back" and hurt the other person as well.[42] On some occasions, it is more prudent to overlook an insult rather than let it upset you.[43] [However, this does not mean that you should allow someone to continually verbally abuse you.]

Don't Swear or Use Filthy Language: Never misuse the name of the Lord your God.[44] Don't use filthy or obscene language or tell "dirty jokes."[45,46] Don't let anything unwholesome come out

---

He [God] mocks proud mockers but
gives grace to the humble.
(Proverbs 3:34)[38]

A mocker resents correction; he will not consult the wise.
(Proverbs 15:12)[39]

Men detest a mocker.
(Proverbs 24:9)[40]

Do not repay evil with evil or insult with insult.
(1 Peter 3:9)[41]

Do not answer a fool according to his folly,
or you will be like him yourself.
(Proverbs 26:4)[42]

A fool shows his annoyance at once,
but a prudent man overlooks an insult.
(Proverbs 12:16)[43]

You shall not misuse the name of the LORD your God, for the LORD will not hold anyone guiltless who misuses his name.
(Exodus 20:7)[44]

But now you must rid yourselves of all such things as these: anger, rage, malice, slander, and filthy language from your lips.
(Colossians 3:8)[45]

Nor should there be obscenity, foolish talk or coarse joking, which are out of place, but rather thanksgiving.
(Ephesians 5:4)[46]

of your mouth.⁴⁷ If you consider yourself to be a religious person but don't keep a tight rein on your tongue, you are deceiving yourself and your "religion is worthless."⁴⁸

Don't Lie: God detests people who tell lies, but He delights in people who are truthful.⁴⁹ If you love life and want to have good things happen to you, then you should watch what you say and avoid telling lies.⁵⁰ In addition, you are also to avoid "deception,"⁵¹,⁵² which is a less obvious form of lying.

If you don't refrain from lying and deception, the consequences can be severe. Scriptures indicate that God "destroys" those who tell lies, and He "abhors" deceitful men.⁵³ Moreover, no one who practices lying or deceit [and is unrepentant] will dwell in God's house or stand in His presence.⁵⁴

> Do not let any unwholesome talk come out of your mouths, but only what is helpful for building others up according to their needs, that it may benefit those who listen.
> **(Ephesians 4:29)**⁴⁷

> If anyone considers himself religious and yet does not keep a tight rein on his tongue, he deceives himself and his religion is worthless.
> **(James 1:26)**⁴⁸

> The LORD detests lying lips, but he delights in men who are truthful.
> **(Proverbs 12:22)**⁴⁹

> Whoever of you loves life and desires to see many good days, keep your tongue from evil and your lips from speaking lies.
> **(Psalm 34:12-13)**⁵⁰

> Do not lie. Do not deceive one another.
> **(Leviticus 19:11)**⁵¹

> Keep me from deceitful ways.
> **(Psalm 119:29)**⁵²

> You destroy those who tell lies; bloodthirsty and deceitful men the LORD abhors.
> **(Psalm 5:6)**⁵³

> No one who practices deceit will dwell in my house; no one who speaks falsely will stand in my presence.
> **(Psalm 101:7)**⁵⁴

Don't Tell Falsehoods: God pays special attention to lies that are targeted at our neighbors (also called "falsehoods"). The Ninth Commandment states: "You shall not give false witness against your neighbor."[55] This is because, when you lie about your neighbor, you can cause him or her great harm.[56] As Christians, we should be especially careful about telling falsehoods about one another, as we are all members of one body.[57]

Some people lie or deceive in order to cheat and steal from others. Although such actions may bring temporary rewards, God cautions us about engaging in dishonest behavior.[58,59] A fortune made through lying can be quickly lost and such ill-gotten gains can prove to be a deadly snare.[60] In the final analysis, it is better to be poor than to be a liar.[61]

Don't Slander: If you speak falsely about someone in order to ruin his or her reputation (i.e., "defame"), this is called *slander*. God specifically commands us not to slander others,[62] and warns

---

"You shall not give false testimony against your neighbor.
(Exodus 20:16)[55]

Like a club or a sword or a sharp arrow is the man who gives false testimony against his neighbor.
(Proverbs 25:18)[56]

Therefore each of you must put off falsehood and speak truthfully to his neighbor, for we are all members of one body.
(Ephesians 4:25)[57]

For the LORD your God detests anyone who does these things, anyone who deals dishonestly.
(Deuteronomy 25:16)[58]

Food gained by fraud tastes sweet to a man, but he ends up with a mouth full of gravel.
(Proverbs 20:17)[59]

A fortune made by a lying tongue is a fleeting vapor and a deadly snare.
(Proverbs 21:6)[60]

Better to be poor than a liar.
(Proverbs 19:22)[61]

"Do not go about spreading slander among your people."
"I am the LORD." **(Leviticus 19:16)**[62]

that He will put to "silence" anyone who slanders his neighbor in secret.[63] King Solomon warns that whoever spreads slander is a fool.[64]

Don't Gossip: Slander is very closely related to *gossip*. When you gossip about someone, you spread rumors about the person "behind his or her back" (that can be harmful or hurtful). Very often, gossip represents a betrayal of something that someone has told another person in confidence.[65,66]

It can be very enticing to listen to another person gossip.[67] However, gossip can prove to be extremely destructive with regard to human relationships. It can break up friendships,[68] and "fuel the fire" of arguments and quarrels.[69] People who are idle (and have too much time on their hands) often gossip and say things they shouldn't say.[70] Avoid godless chatter.[71]

Whoever slanders his neighbor in secret, him will I put to silence.
(Psalm 101:5)[63]

Whoever spreads slander is a fool.
(Proverbs 10:18)[64]

A gossip betrays a confidence,
but a trustworthy man keeps a secret.
(Proverbs 11:13)[65]

A gossip betrays a confidence; so avoid a man who talks too much.
(Proverbs 20:19)[66]

The words of a gossip are like choice morsels;
they go down to a man's inmost parts.
(Proverbs 18:8)[67]

A gossip separates close friends.
(Proverbs 16:28)[68]

Without wood a fire goes out; without gossip a quarrel dies down.
(Proverbs 26:20)[69]

Besides, they [young widowers] get into the habit of being idle
and going about from house to house. And not only do
they become idlers, but also gossips and busybodies,
saying things they ought not to say.
(1 Timothy 5:13)[70]

Avoid godless chatter, because those who indulge in it
will become more and more ungodly.
(2 Timothy 2:16)[71]

Don't Keep Bringing Up The Past: If the person you are talking to has sinned against you, but has genuinely and truly repented, you should forgive him/her and stop bringing up the past offense.[72,73] Love keeps no record of wrongs.[74]

God's Guidance

What to Say:

Be truthful: It pleases God when we are truthful,[75,76] and when we answer honestly.[77] A person who tells lies may benefit temporarily, but "truthful lips" endure forever.[78] If you tell lies or are deceitful, you should repent and pray that God will remove this sin from your heart.[79,80]

Be kind and compassionate to one another, forgiving each other, just as in Christ God forgave you.
(Ephesians 4:32)[72]

Bear with each other and forgive whatever grievances you may have against one another. Forgive as the Lord forgave you.
(Colossians 3:13)[73]

Love is patient, love is kind...it keeps no record of wrongs.
(1 Corinthians 13: 4-5)[74]

O LORD, do not your eyes look for truth?
(Jeremiah 5:3)[75]

Surely you desire truth in the inner parts; you teach me wisdom in the inmost place.
(Psalm 51:6)[76]

An honest answer is like a kiss on the lips.
(Proverbs 24:26)[77]

Truthful lips endure forever, but a lying tongue lasts only a moment.
(Proverbs 12:19)[78]

Keep falsehood and lies far from me.
(Proverbs 30:8)[79]

Keep me from deceitful ways.
(Psalm 119: 29)[80]

If you are tempted to lie or deceive, you should remember that the devil is a liar, and the "father of all lies."[81] Resist the devil, and he will flee from you.[82]

<u>Say Nice Things</u>: Kind and pleasant words can be very powerful, and can help heal any situation. Choose your words carefully; they can serve as beautiful gifts—like "apples of gold in settings of silver."[83] They can be "sweet to the soul and healing to the bones."[84] And they can aid in the process of teaching and learning.[85]

<u>Be Happy, Cheerful, Joyful</u>: You can set the emotional tone for good communication. As much as depends on you, strive to be happy,[86,87] cheerful,[88,89] and joyful.[90]

When he [the devil] lies, he speaks his native language, for he is a liar and the father of lies.
(John 8:44)[81]

Resist the devil, and he will flee from you.
(James 4:7)[82]

A word aptly spoken is like apples of gold in settings of silver
(Proverbs 25:11)[83]

Pleasant words are a honeycomb, sweet to the soul and healing to the bones.
(Proverbs 16:24)[84]

Pleasant words promote instruction.
(Proverbs 16:21)[85]

I know that there is nothing better for men than to be happy and do good while they live.
(Ecclesiastes 3:12)[86]

But may the righteous be glad and rejoice before God; may they be happy and joyful.
(Psalm 68:3)[87]

The cheerful heart has a continual feast.
(Proverbs 15:15)[88]

A cheerful heart is good medicine.
(Proverbs 17:22)[89]

Encourage One Another: Encourage each other daily, and build each other up.[91,92] Spur one another toward love and good deeds.[93] Nourish one another[94] and let God's Word guide your speech.[95]

Finally, strive to live a righteous and holy life, and let everything that comes out of your mouth reflect the faith you have in Jesus Christ. The mouth of a righteous man can be a "fountain of life."[96] Be peaceable and considerate, and show true humility toward all men.[97]

Be joyful always; pray continually; give thanks in
all circumstances, for this is God's
will for you in Christ Jesus.
(1 Thessalonians 5:16-18)[90]

But encourage one another daily, as long as it is called
Today, so that none of you may be hardened
by sin's deceitfulness.
(Hebrews 3:13)[91]

Therefore encourage one another and build
each other up, just as in fact you are doing.
(1 Thessalonians 5:11)[92]

And let us consider how we may spur one
another on toward love and good deeds.
(Hebrews 10:24)[93]

The lips of the righteous nourish many.
(Proverbs 10:21)[94]

I have hidden your word in my heart that
I might not sin against you.
(Psalm 119:11)[95]

The mouth of the righteous is a fountain of life.
(Proverbs 15:4)[96]

Remind the people...to slander no one, to be
peaceable and considerate, and show true
humility toward all men.
(Titus 3:2)[97]

As much as is possible, strive to live in peace and harmony with everyone; be sympathetic and compassionate.[98] Regardless of your situation, conduct yourself in a manner that is worthy of the gospel of Christ.[99] In the end, those who walk uprightly will find peace,[100] and the righteous will "shine like the sun" in the kingdom of heaven.[101]

> Finally, all of you, live in harmony with one another;
> be sympathetic, love as brothers,
> be compassionate and humble.
> **(1 Peter 3:8)**[98]
>
> Whatever happens, conduct yourselves in a manner
> worthy of the gospel of Christ.
> **(Philippians 1:27)**[99]
>
> Those who walk uprightly enter into peace.
> **(Isaiah 57:2)**[100]
>
> *Then the righteous will shine like the sun in the kingdom
> of their Father. He who has ears, let him hear.*
> **(Matthew 13:43)**[101]

Lesson 11

Death and Dying

"No one has power over the day of his death."
(Ecclesiastes 8:8)

Death: the act of dying; the end of physical life

For Christians, death is nothing to fear. Death is merely the end of our life on earth and the beginning of our life in heaven. If you have lost a loved one, or if you are facing death yourself, pray that God, in His infinite love and mercy, will forgive your sins and accept you into heaven. Jesus Himself has gone ahead of you to prepare a place for those who believe in Him and are saved by His sacrifice on the cross.

Synopsis

If you are a Christian, you should not fear death.[1,2] The day that you first believed in Jesus Christ is the day that you crossed over from death to life.[3-5]

Our God is a God who saves; from the Sovereign LORD
comes escape from death.
(Psalm 68:20)[1]

I will ransom them from the power of the grave; I will redeem
them from death. Where, O death, are your plagues?
Where, O grave, is your destruction?
(Hosea 13:14)[2]

He who has the Son has life; he who does not have
the Son of God does not have life.
(1 John 5:12)[3]

*I tell you the truth, whoever hears my word and believes him
who sent me has eternal life and will not be condemned;
he has crossed over from death to life.*
(John 5:26)[4]

For to me, to live is Christ and to die is gain.
(Philippians 1:21)[5]

All human beings have a physical body and a soul (also called "spirit").[6] The physical body of every human being is going to die at some point in time.[7,8] The days of our physical existence on earth are numbered by God, and we cannot add to them or subtract from them.[9] No one has the power to control the day of his physical death.[10]

Death first entered into the world with the disobedience of Adam in the Garden of Eden; but just as Adam brought death to the world, Jesus Christ brought life.[11] The resurrection of Jesus from the dead, following His crucifixion on the cross, gives hope for all who believe in Him.[12] If Jesus Christ had not risen from the dead, then death would be the end of existence for everyone, even for believers.[13]

---

*Do not be afraid of those who kill the body
but cannot kill the soul.*
(Matthew 10:28)[6]

Death is the destiny of every man;
the living should take this to heart.
(Ecclesiastes 7:2)[7]

There is a time for everything, and a season for every activity
under heaven: a time to be born and a time to die...
(Ecclesiastes 3:1-2)[8]

Man's days are determined; you have decreed the number
of his months and have set limits he cannot exceed.
(Job 14:5)[9]

No man has power over the wind to contain it; so no
one has power over the day of his death.
(Ecclesiastes 8:8)[10]

For since death came through a man, the resurrection of
the dead comes also through a man. For as in Adam
all die, so in Christ all will be made alive.
(1 Corinthians 15:21-22)[11]

Praise be to the God and Father of our Lord Jesus Christ!
In his great mercy he has given us new birth into
a living hope through the resurrection of
Jesus Christ from the dead.
(1 Peter 1:3)[12]

Fortunately, Christ has indeed been raised from the dead[14] and those who believe in Him are promised eternal life in heaven.[15] When we die, our physical body will decay and go back to dust.[16] Our spirit (or soul) will go immediately to heaven.[17-19] For unbelievers, their souls will go immediately to hell, where they will await the final judgment day.[20]

And if Christ has not been raised, our preaching is useless and so is your faith...Then those also who have fallen asleep in Christ are lost.
(1 Corinthians 15:14,18)[13]

But Christ has indeed been raised from the dead, the firstfruits of those who have fallen asleep.
(1 Corinthians 15:20)[14]

For God so loved the world that he gave his one and only Son, that whoever believes in him shall not perish but have eternal life.
(John 3:16)[15]

For dust you are and to dust you will return.
(Genesis 3:19)[16]

Jesus called out with a loud voice, *"Father, into your hands I commit my spirit."* When he had said this, he breathed his last.
(Luke 23:46)[17]

Then he said, "Jesus, remember me when you come into your kingdom." Jesus answered him, *"I tell you the truth, today you will be with me in paradise."*
(Luke 23:42-43)[17]

For to me, to live is Christ and to die is gain...I am torn between the two: I desire to depart and be with Christ, which is better by far; but it is more necessary for you that I remain in the body.
(Philippians 1:21,23-24)[19]

For if God did not spare angels when they sinned, but sent them to hell, putting them into gloomy dungeons to be held for judgment...then the Lord knows how to rescue godly men from trials and to hold the unrighteous for the day of judgment, while continuing their punishment.
(2 Peter 2:4,9)[20]

At some future point in time, Jesus will return to this earth (the second coming) for a final judgment.[21,22] Spirit and flesh will be reunited and we will receive our glorified bodies.[23] These bodies will be different to our earthly bodies, and they will no longer decay or die.[24] They will resemble the body that Christ received when He was resurrected from the dead, and they will last forever in heaven.[25]

Following the second coming of Christ, the people who believe in Jesus will live for eternity with Christ, even though they have died in the flesh. In a very real sense, whoever lives and believes in Christ will never die (that is, will never be "spiritually dead" and lose eternity).[26]

> Just as man is destined to die once, and after that to face judgment, so Christ was sacrificed once to take away the sins of many people; and he will appear a second time, not to bear sin, but to bring salvation to those who are waiting for him.
> **(Hebrews 9:27-28)**[21]

> For we must all appear before the judgment seat of Christ, that each one may receive what is due him for the things done while in the body, whether good or bad.
> **(2 Corinthians 5:10)**[22]

> But our citizenship is in heaven. And we eagerly await a Savior from there, the Lord Jesus Christ, who, by the power that enables him to bring everything under his control, will transform our lowly bodies so that they will be like his glorious body.
> **(Philippians 3:20-21)**[23]

> So will it be with the resurrection of the dead. The body that is sown is perishable, it is raised imperishable... It is sown a natural body, it is raised a spiritual body.
> **(1 Corinthians 15:42,44)**[24]

> And just as we have borne the likeness of the earthly man, so shall we bear the likeness of the man from heaven.
> **(1 Corinthians 15:49)**[25]

> *I am the resurrection and the life. He who believes in me will live, even though he dies; and whoever lives and believes in me will never die.*
> **(John 11: 25-26)**[26]

No one knows the hour or the day that Christ will return to this world, only God the Father.[27] Therefore, it is critically important that we accept Jesus Christ as our Lord and Savior and repent of our sins.[28] For if Jesus returns to this world while we are still alive, we will be judged and we will either spend eternity in heaven or eternity in hell (separated from God).[29]

If you are a believer in Christ, death should not be fearful; only our physical body dies, not our spirit (or soul).[30] Jesus Christ has defeated death.[31-34] Jesus Himself has gone ahead of us to prepare a place for us in heaven.[35] Physical death will not separate us from

---

No one knows about that day or hour, not even the angels in heaven, nor the Son, but only the Father.
(Matthew 24:36)[27]

The kingdom of God is near. Repent and believe the good news!
(Mark 1:15)[28]

This will happen when the Lord Jesus is revealed from heaven... He will punish those who do not know God and do not obey the gospel of our Lord Jesus. They will be punished with everlasting destruction and shut out from the presence of the Lord.
(2 Thessalonians 1:7-9)[29]

Do not be afraid of those who kill the body but cannot kill the soul.
(Matthew 10:28)[30]

For he must reign until he has put all his enemies under his feet. The last enemy to be destroyed is death.
(1 Corinthians 15:25-26)[31]

We believe that Jesus died and rose again and so we believe that God will bring with Jesus those who have fallen asleep in him.
(1 Thessalonians 4:14)[32]

For this very reason, Christ died and returned to life so that he might be the Lord of both the dead and the living.
(Romans 14:9)[33]

Our God is a God who saves; from the Sovereign LORD comes escape from death.
(Psalm 68:20)[34]

Do not let your hearts be troubled...In my Father's house are many rooms...I am going there to prepare a place for you.
(John 14:1-2)[35]

the love of God.[36] The apostle Paul went so far as to say that he would prefer to be "absent from the body and to be at home with the Lord."[37]

If you are having trouble coping with death, try focusing your thoughts firmly on heaven. In heaven, we will be with Jesus,[38,39] and see Him face to face.[40,41] He wants us to live there forever with Him and experience His glory.[42]

> For I am persuaded that neither death nor life, neither angels nor demons, neither the present nor the future, nor any powers, neither height nor depth, nor anything else in all creation, will be able to separate us from the love of God that is in Christ Jesus our Lord.
> **(Romans 8:38-39)**[36]
>
> We are confident, I say, and would prefer to be away from the body and at home with the Lord.
> **(2 Corinthians 5:8)**[37]
>
> *And if I go and prepare a place for you, I will come back and take you to be with me that you also may be where I am.*
> **(John 14:3)**[38]
>
> But God will redeem my life from the grave; he will surely take me to himself.
> **(Psalm 49:15)**[39]
>
> I see heaven open and the Son of Man standing at the right hand of God.
> **(Acts 7:56)**[40]
>
> And I—in righteousness I will see your face; when I awake, I will be satisfied with seeing your likeness.
> **(Psalm 17:15)**[41]
>
> *Father, I want those you have given me to be with me where I am, and to see my glory, the glory you have given me because you loved me before the creation of the world.*
> **(John 17:24)**[42]

If you have a loved one who has died who is an infant, rest assured that he or she will be in heaven.[43,44]

If your loved one is a believer who dies, take comfort that he or she is now with our Lord and Savior in heaven.[45,46]

God's Guidance

It is difficult to imagine how beautiful and wonderful heaven will be. It will not be like anything we have ever seen, or heard, or conceived of, here on earth.[47] The apostle John describes heaven as being a city made of pure gold, as pure as glass, with foundations of the city walls decorated with every kind of precious stone.[48,49]

See that you do not look down on one of these little ones. For I tell you that their angels in heaven always see the face of my Father in heaven.
(Matthew 18:10)[43]

In the same way your Father in heaven is not willing that any of these little ones should be lost.
(Matthew 18:14)[44]

For to me, to live is Christ and to die is gain...I desire to depart and be with Christ, which is better by far...
(Philippians 1:21,23)[45]

Those who walk uprightly enter into peace; they find rest as they lie in death.
(Isaiah 57:2)[46]

No eye has seen, no ear has heard, no mind has conceived what God has prepared for those who love him.
(1 Corinthians 2:9)[47]

The wall was made of jasper, and the city of pure gold, as pure as glass. The foundations of the city walls were decorated with every kind of precious stone.
(Revelation 21:18-19)[48]

The twelve gates were twelve pearls, each gate made of a single pearl. The great street of the city was of pure gold, like transparent glass.
(Revelation 21:21)[49]

Although unimaginable, heaven will be familiar to us in many ways. For example, we know that we will have bodies in heaven (our "glorified" bodies) and that we will eat and drink, just as we did here on earth.[50] We will have eyes and ears and be able to see and hear.[51,52] Unlike our life on earth, there will be no more death or mourning, or crying or pain.[52] There will be no sin in heaven and nothing there will be impure.[53]

There will be no darkness or night in heaven, and no sun or moon.[54,55] The glory of God will give heaven its light.[54]

Finally, as we face death, one of the most comforting Scriptures in the entire Bible can be found in Psalm 23:

"Even though I walk through the valley of the shadow of death, I will fear no evil, for you are with me; your rod and your staff, they comfort me. You prepare a table before me in the presence of my enemies. You anoint my head with oil; my cup overflows. Surely goodness and love will follow me all the days of my life, and I will dwell in the house of the Lord forever." (Psalm 23:4-6)

And I confer on you a kingdom, just as my Father conferred one on me, so that you may eat and drink at my table in my kingdom and sit on thrones, judging the twelve tribes of Israel.
(Luke 22:29-30)[50]

The sound of weeping and of crying will be heard in it no more.
(Isaiah 65:19)[51]

He will wipe every tear from their eyes. There will be no more death or mourning or crying or pain, for the old order of things has passed away.
(Revelation 21:4)[52]

Nothing impure will ever enter it.
(Revelation 21:27)[53]

There will be no more night. They will not need the light of a lamp or the light of the sun, for the Lord God will give them light. And they will reign for ever and ever.
(Revelation 22:5)[54]

The city does not need the sun or the moon to shine on it, for the glory of God gives it light, and the Lamb is its lamp.
(Revelation 21:23)[55]

Lesson 12

Depression

"But as for me, I will always have hope;
I will praise you more and more."
(Psalm 71:14)

Depression: a pessimistic state of mind that affects
thoughts, emotions, and behavior

Depression is one of the most common mental health problems in the entire world. People who are depressed feel sad, blue, or downhearted. They have lost their energy for life, and feel hopeless, helpless, worthless, and guilty. Fortunately, God's Word is filled with inspiration for people who are feeling depressed.

Synopsis

Hopeless:

One of the triggers for depression is the false belief that your situation is hopeless. If you are a Christian, this is a lie that is contradicted throughout the Bible.

If you are feeling hopeless about life, try turning to God's Word for guidance and direction. Everything written in the Bible was written to teach and encourage so that we might have hope.[1,2]

> For everything that was written in the past was written to
> teach us, so that through endurance and the
> encouragement of the Scriptures
> we might have hope.
> **(Romans 15:4)**[1]
>
> You are my refuge and my shield;
> I have put my hope in your word.
> **(Psalm 119:114)**[2]

Throughout the Bible, we are reminded that God alone is the source of our hope.[3] In fact, the Scriptures refer to God as the "God of hope."[4]

When Jesus Christ died on the cross and was raised from the dead, He became a living hope for all of us.[5] Because of Christ's sacrifice, we can now rest in the assurance that when we die, this is not the end of life, but only the beginning of eternity with Christ Jesus.[6]

If you are feeling downcast and gloomy about life, step back and put things in perspective.[7] Put your hope in God's promise of His glorious inheritance—eternal salvation and life ever after in heaven.[8] The Lord is good to those who place their hope in Him—to the one who seeks Him.[9] If you are feeling hopeless, turn back to God.

> Find rest, O my soul, in God alone; my hope comes from him.
> **(Psalm 62:5)**[3]
>
> May the God of hope fill you with all joy and peace
> as you trust in him, so that you may overflow with hope by
> the power of the Holy Spirit.
> **(Romans 15:13)**[4]
>
> Praise be to the God and Father of our Lord Jesus Christ!
> In his great mercy he has given us new birth into a living
> hope through the resurrection of Jesus Christ from the dead.
> **(1 Peter 1:3)**[5]
>
> God has given us eternal life, and this life is in his Son.
> **(1 John 5:11)**[6]
>
> Why are you downcast, O my soul? Why so disturbed
> within me? Put your hope in God, for I will yet praise him,
> my Savior and my God.
> **(Psalm 43:5)**[7]
>
> I pray also that the eyes of your heart may be enlightened in
> order that you may know the hope to which he has called you,
> the riches of his glorious inheritance in the saints, and his
> incomparably great power for us who believe.
> **(Ephesians 1:18-19)**[8]
>
> The LORD is good to those whose hope is in him,
> to the one who seeks him.
> **(Lamentations 3:25)**[9]

Regardless of your current situation, God's plans are for you to prosper and to have hope.[10]

If you put your hope in God, you will never be disappointed,[11] or put to shame.[12] Be patient in your afflictions and faithful in prayer.[13] Even if you are suffering, this experience can help develop character and ultimately lead to hope,[14] as you rest in God's unfailing love.[15]

As you turn to God for hope, be careful that you don't listen to the "false hopes" given by the world.[16] Watch what you say to yourself. Refuse to tell yourself your situation is hopeless,[17] and don't focus

---

"For I know the plans I have for you," declares the LORD,
"plans to prosper you and not to harm you,
plans to give you hope and a future."
(Jeremiah 29:11)[10]

Those who hope in me will not be disappointed.
(Isaiah 49:23)[11]

No one whose hope is in you will ever be put to shame.
(Psalm 25:3)[12]

Be joyful in hope, patient in affliction, faithful in prayer.
(Romans 12:12)[13]

But we also rejoice in our sufferings, because we know that suffering produces perseverance; perseverance, character; and character, hope.
(Romans 5:3)[14]

May your unfailing love rest upon us,
O LORD, even as we put our hope in you.
(Psalm 33:22)[15]

This is what the LORD Almighty says: "Do not listen to what the prophets are prophesying to you; they fill you with false hopes. They speak visions from their own minds, not from the mouth of the LORD.
(Jeremiah 23:16)[16]

You were wearied by all your ways, but you would not say, "It is hopeless." You found renewal of your strength, and so you did not faint.
(Isaiah 57:10)[17]

on your afflictions—focus on the Lord's compassion and love.[18] God knows your needs; you have not been forgotten.[19]

In the final analysis, only those who do not know God should feel hopeless.[20,21] For Christians, there is always hope.[22,23]

> *"But those who hope in the LORD will renew their strength. They will soar on wings like eagles; they will run and not grow weary, they will walk and not be faint."* (Isaiah 40:31)

Helpless:

If you are feeling helpless or powerless, turn to the Lord and His strength.[24] Remember that you have the Creator of the universe on your side.[25] He is the God who performs miracles and displays His power among the people.[26] Nothing is too hard for God.[27]

I remember my affliction and my wandering, the bitterness and the gall. I well remember them, and my soul is downcast within me. Yet this I call to mind and therefore I have hope: Because of the LORD's great love we are not consumed,
for his compassions never fail.
(Lamentations 3:19-22)[18]

But the needy will not always be forgotten,
nor the hope of the afflicted ever perish.
(Psalm 9:18)[19]

Such is the destiny of all who forget God;
so perishes the hope of the godless.
(Job 8:13)[20]

When a wicked man dies, his hope perishes;
all he expected from his power comes to nothing.
(Proverbs 11:7)[21]

But as for me, I will always have hope;
I will praise you more and more.
(Psalm 71:14)[22]

There is surely a future hope for you
and your hope will not be cut off.
(Proverbs 23:18)[23]

Be strong in the Lord and in His mighty power.[28] The Lord knows how to rescue godly men from trials.[29] If you are feeling helpless, try turning to God; the prayers of a righteous man are powerful and effective.[30] If we ask anything in God's name, He promises to provide.[31]

Worthless:

If you are feeling worthless, consider that you are made in God's image,[32,33] and that God loves you more than you can ever know or understand.[34,35]

It is God who arms me with strength
and makes my way perfect.
(Psalm 18:32)[24]

In his hand is the life of every creature and the
breath of all mankind.
(Job 12:10)[25]

You are the God who performs miracles;
you display your power among the peoples.
(Psalm 77:14)[26]

Ah, Sovereign LORD, you have made the heavens and
the earth by your great power and outstretched
arm. Nothing is too hard for you.
(Jeremiah 32:17)[27]

Finally, be strong in the Lord and in his mighty power.
(Ephesians 6:10)[28]

The Lord knows how to rescue godly men from trials.
(2 Peter 2:9)[29]

The prayer of a righteous man is powerful and effective.
(James 5:16)[30]

*I tell you the truth, my Father will give you
whatever you ask in my name.*
(John 16:23)[31]

So God created man in his own image, in the image of God he
created him; male and female he created them.
(Genesis 1:27)[32]

God is our Heavenly Father,[36] and we are His offspring.[37] He has made us "a little lower than the heavenly beings," and He crowns us with glory and honor.[38] He counts the very hairs on our heads.[39] When we follow His commandments, Jesus Christ, who holds the keys to eternal life, even calls us His "friend."[40]

> And just as we have borne the likeness of the earthly man, so shall we bear the likeness of the man from heaven.
> **(1 Corinthians 15:49)**[33]

> How precious is your unfailing love!
> **(Psalm 36:7)**[34]

> I will sing of the Lord's great love forever.
> **(Psalm 89:1)**[35]

> O Lord, you are our Father. We are the clay, you are the potter.
> **(Isaiah 64:8)**[36]

> We are his offspring.
> **(Acts 17:28)**[37]

> You made him a little lower than the heavenly beings and crowned him with glory and honor.
> **(Psalm 8:5)**[38]

> *Indeed, the very hairs of your head are all numbered.*
> **(Luke 12:7)**[39]

> *You are my friends if you do what I command. I no longer call you servants, because a servant does not know his master's business. Instead, I have called you friends, for everything that I learned from my Father I have made known to you.*
> **(John 15:14-15)**[40]

> Has not God chosen those who are poor in the eyes of the world to be rich in faith and to inherit the kingdom promised those who love him?
> **(James 2:5)**[41]

You don't have to be rich or successful to be worthy in God's eyes,[41-43] and you don't have to be perfect.[44] Everyone sins,[45] and everyone makes mistakes.[46] If you have broken God's commands, repent[47] and turn back to God.[48] He will receive you with open arms.[49]

Joyless:

People with depression have a difficult time experiencing joy and happiness. They have convinced themselves that there is nothing at all in this world in which to be happy. No matter what happens in their lives, they tend to look at the world "through dark colored glasses," and focus on the negative aspects of their experiences.

Wealth is worthless in the day of wrath
but righteousness delivers from death.
(Proverbs 11:4)[42]

Whoever trusts in his riches will fall,
but the righteous will thrive like a green leaf.
(Proverbs 11:28)[43]

There is not a righteous man on earth who does
what is right and never sins.
(Ecclesiastes 7:20)[44]

For all have sinned and fall short of the glory of God.
(Romans 3:23)[45]

No one is good except God alone.
(Mark 10:18)[46]

Come back to your senses as you ought, and stop sinning.
(1 Corinthians 15:34)[47]

Let him turn to the LORD, and he will have mercy on him,
and to our God, for he will freely pardon.
(Isaiah 55:7)[48]

The eternal God is your refuge, and underneath
are the everlasting arms.
(Deuteronomy 33:27)[49]

Christians who are joyless have lost perspective in life. They have let their own inadequacies or their own experiences blind them from the truth of the gospel and the source of all joy—our relationship with Jesus Christ our Lord and Savior, with God the Father who sent Him, and with the Holy Spirit who dwells within us.

As Christians, there are plenty of things about which to be joyful. If you are depressed and find it difficult experiencing joy, try meditating on God's incredible love for you.[50,51] Not only did God send His son to die for us, He sent the Holy Spirit to testify that we are His children.[52]

The God of the universe created us and gave us life.[53] We can rejoice in that fact and be glad for every day that God has given us on this planet.[54,55]

As the Father has loved me, so have I loved you.
Now remain in my love.
(John 15:9)[50]

May the Lord direct your hearts into God's love
and Christ's perseverance.
(2 Thessalonians 3:5)[51]

The Spirit himself testifies with our spirit that
we are God's children.
(Romans 8:16)[52]

For in him we live and move and have our being.
(Acts 17:28)[53]

I will praise you forever for what you have done.
(Psalm 52:9)[54]

This is the day the Lord has made;
let us rejoice and be glad in it.
(Psalm 118:24)[55]

Be joyful always, pray continuously, give thanks in all circumstances, for this is God's will for you in Christ Jesus.
(1 Thessalonians 5:16-18)[56]

Regardless of what has happened to us, we can still be joyful[56] and give thanks to the Lord for what He has done.[57] Sing joyfully to the Lord,[58] sing praise to Him; tell of all His wonderful acts.[59]

Energyless:

People who are depressed often feel weak and energyless. They have lost their zeal and enthusiasm for life. They find it difficult to "get going" and get things done.

If you are feeling weak and depleted in energy, turn to God for help. He gives strength to the weary, and increases the power of the weak.[60]

Draw on His strength, and seek His help.[61] If you are weary and burdened, He invites you to come to Him to find rest.[62] Pray for God to refresh your heart.[63]

Give thanks to the LORD, for he is good.
His love endures forever.
(Psalm 136:1)[57]

Sing joyfully to the LORD, you righteous;
it is fitting for the upright to praise him.
(Psalm 33:1)[58]

Sing to him, sing praise to him; tell of all his wonderful acts.
(Psalm 105:2)[59]

He gives strength to the weary and increases
the power of the weak.
(Isaiah 40:29)[60]

Look to the LORD and his strength; seek his face always.
(Psalm 105:4)[61]

*Come to me, all you who are weary and burdened,
and I will give you rest.*
(Matthew 11:28)[62]

Refresh my heart in Christ.
(Philemon 1:20)[63]

Once you have been re-energized (or even if you are still feeling tired), one of the best things you can do to help yourself is to "get up" and "take action." If you are physically able, start taking walks and getting exercise; remember, your body is the temple of God, and you should take care of it.[64]

To the extent that you are physically able, go and help someone; helping others will serve to get your mind off your own problems. God does not want us to simply talk about our faith—He wants to see it in action.[65,66] Regardless of how tired you may feel, you can always find some way to reach out and help others. By so doing, you will be showing God's love[67] and helping yourself at the same time.[68]

Guilty:

People who are depressed often feel that they have committed some horrible act for which they can never be forgiven. As a result, their guilt is overwhelming. This is one of the biggest lies they can believe.

Apart from the special case of blasphemy, the Bible tells us that there is absolutely nothing that God will not forgive if we confess

---

> Do you not know that your body is a temple of the Holy Spirit, who is in you, whom you have received from God? You are not your own; you were bought at a price.
> Therefore honor God with your body.
> **(1 Corinthians 6:19-20)**[64]
>
> Dear children, let us not love with words or tongue but with actions and in truth.
> **(1 John 3:18)**[65]
>
> Do not merely listen to the word, and so deceive yourselves.
> Do what it says.
> **(James 1:22)**[66]
>
> Love one another deeply, from the heart.
> **(1 Peter 1:22)**[67]
>
> No one has ever seen God; but if we love one another, God lives in us and his love is made complete in us.
> **(1 John 4:12)**[68]

our sin and repent. Everyone who believes in Christ receives forgiveness of sins through His name.[69]

If you believe in Christ, there is no longer any condemnation for sin[70]—none whatsoever! This is precisely why Christ came to this earth to die for us, so that we could be reconciled with God. He laid down His life for us to take away our sins,[71] so that we could live forever with Him in heaven.

If you have sinned, there may certainly be unpleasant consequences in this world for what you have done.[72] A man reaps what he sows.[73] Fortunately, if you are a Christian, the consequences of your sin will not block your entrance to heaven.[74,75] After all, Christ came to this earth to save sinners, just like you and me.[76]

Everyone who believes in him
receives forgiveness through his name.
(Acts 10:43)[69]

Therefore, there is now no condemnation for those who are in Christ Jesus, because through Christ Jesus the law of the Spirit of life set me free from the law of sin and death.
(Romans 8:1-2)[70]

*I am the good shepherd. The good shepherd
lays down his life for the sheep.*
(John 10:11)[71]

There will be trouble and distress for
every human being who does evil.
(Romans 2:9)[72]

Do not be deceived: God cannot be mocked.
A man reaps what he sows.
(Galatians 6:7)[73]

God demonstrates his own love for us in this:
While we were still sinners, Christ died for us.
(Romans 5:8)[74]

God was reconciling the world to himself in Christ,
not counting men's sins against them.
(2 Corinthians 5:19)[75]

Try not to dwell on any wrongs you may have committed. Instead, confess your sins and then turn them over to God—knowing that they will never be counted against you.[77] If you have harmed someone, take time to confess your sin to him or her.[78]

Then, as far as possible, take any action you can that will lead to peace and restoration of the relationship.[79,80] If you are blocked from taking action, then pray for the person you have offended,[81] and ask for God's wisdom and guidance on how to proceed.

Finally, when you commit a sin you "grieve the Holy Spirit" who lives within you.[82] Therefore, it is only natural that you will experience temporary sorrow and guilt for what you have done. However, your guilt should be short-lived, as you move on to accept the

---

> For all have sinned and fall short of the glory of God,
> and are justified freely by his grace through the
> redemption that came by Christ Jesus.
> **(Romans 3:23-24)**[76]

> If we confess our sins, he is faithful and just and will forgive
> us our sins and purify us from all unrighteousness.
> **(1 John 1:9)**[77]

> Confess your sins to each other and pray for each other
> so that you may be healed.
> **(James 5:16)**[78]

> Let us therefore make every effort to what leads
> to peace and to mutual edification.
> **(Romans 14:19)**[79]

> If it is possible, as far as it depends on you,
> live at peace with everyone.
> **(Romans 12:18)**[80]

> And pray in the Spirit on all occasions
> with all kinds of prayers and requests.
> **(Ephesians 6:18)**[81]

> And do not grieve the Holy Spirit of God,
> with whom you were sealed for the day of redemption.
> **(Ephesians 4:30)**[82]

awesome gift of forgiveness that was paid in full by Jesus Christ on the cross of Calvary.[83]

He himself bore our sins in his body on the tree,
so that we might die to sins and live for righteousness;
by his wounds we have been healed.
(1 Peter 2:24)[83]

To receive an audio recording of:

"Overcoming Depression"

(Scriptures for depression read by Dr. Brian Campbell),

Please Visit:

Counseling4Christians.com

Lesson 13

Divorce

"I hate divorce," says the Lord God of Israel."
(Malachi 2:16)

Divorce: the legal dissolution of a marriage

Divorce rates are soaring worldwide—even among Christians. The impact of divorce can be felt throughout the family system and the damaging effects can extend from one generation to the next. God's Word takes a very firm stance on divorce. It is only permitted under very narrowly defined circumstances.

Synopsis

The Lord God Almighty hates divorce.[1] He allowed divorce at only one point in history—when Moses and his people walked this earth.[2] Prior to that time (from the point of creation to the time of Moses), divorce was not permitted.[2] Interestingly, the Bible reveals that the exception God made for the followers of Moses (i.e., divorce) did not remain for long.

When Jesus began His ministry on this earth, He proclaimed to His followers that divorce was no longer permitted.[3] There was

---

"I hate divorce," says the Lord God of Israel.
(Malachi 2:16)[1]

Moses permitted you to divorce your wives because your hearts were hard. But it was not this way from the beginning.
(Matthew 19:8)[2]

It has been said, "Anyone who divorces his wife must give her a certificate of divorce." But I tell you that anyone who divorces his wife, except for marital unfaithfulness, causes her to become an adulteress, and anyone who marries the divorced woman commits adultery.
(Matthew 5:31-32)[3]

only one exception, and that was for "marital unfaithfulness" (sexual intercourse outside of marriage).[3] If a man or woman got divorced for any other reason, and then got married again, Jesus said he or she would be committing adultery;[4,5] also, if a man were to marry a divorced woman, he would be committing adultery.[6]

Later on, the apostle Paul reaffirmed what Jesus had proclaimed.[7] In addition, Paul provided further information and clarification regarding divorce. For example, in the case where a believer is married to an unbeliever, if the unbeliever wants to stay in the marriage, then the believer is not permitted to divorce.[8,9]

I tell you that anyone who divorces his wife,
except for marital unfaithfulness,
and marries another woman commits adultery.
(Matthew 19:9)[4]

And if she divorces her husband and marries another man,
she commits adultery.
(Mark 10:12)[5]

Anyone who divorces his wife and marries another woman
commits adultery, and the man who marries a divorced
woman commits adultery.
(Luke 16:18)[6]

To the married I give this command (not I, but the Lord):
A wife must not separate from her husband. But if
she does, she must remain unmarried or else be
reconciled to her husband. And a husband
must not divorce his wife.
(1 Corinthians 7:10-11)[7]

If any brother has a wife who is not a believer
and she is willing to live with him, he must not divorce her.
(1 Corinthians 7:12)[8]

And if a woman has a husband who is not a believer and
he is willing to live with her, she must not divorce him.
(1 Corinthians 7:13)[9]

However, if an unbeliever leaves the marriage, then the believer is no longer bound in such circumstances (and is permitted to divorce).[10]

Thus, the Scriptures reveal only two exceptions where divorce is permissible, namely: "marital unfaithfulness,"[3] and abandonment by an unbeliever.[10] If you divorce for "non-biblical" reasons, God commands that you stay unmarried or else reconcile with your former spouse.[7] Even the process of "separation" (as an alternative to divorce) appears biblically questionable as a long-term strategy or permanent solution for dealing with difficult marriages.[7,11]

Finally, in the instance where a man or woman is married and the spouse dies, he or she is free to marry again, as long as the other person is a believer.[12]

God's Guidance

If you are divorced, thinking of getting a divorce, or considering marrying someone who has had a divorce, you should seek godly counsel. The situations surrounding divorce are often complex and typically require thoughtful prayer,[13] biblical guidance,[14] and

> But if the unbeliever leaves, let him do so. A believing man or woman is not bound in such circumstances; God has called us to live in peace.
> **(1 Corinthians 7:15)**[10]
>
> Do not deprive each other except by mutual consent and for a time, so that you may devote yourselves to prayer. Then come together again so that Satan will not tempt you because of your lack of self-control.
> **(1 Corinthians 7:5)**[11]
>
> A woman is bound to her husband as long as he lives. But if her husband dies, she is free to marry anyone else she wishes, but he must belong to the Lord.
> **(1 Corinthians 7:39)**[12]
>
> Is any one of you in trouble? He should pray.
> **(James 5:13)**[13]
>
> Your statutes are my delight; they are my counselors.
> **(Psalm 119:24)**[14]

wise counsel.[15] As you seek guidance, study God's commandments and turn to the Holy Spirit for help—the great Counselor, "who will guide you into all truth."[16,17]

Finally, if you are in a divorce situation, try not to be argumentative.[18] And if you are divorced and have children, make every effort to provide for them financially, and for your ex-spouse (if necessary); if you do not provide for your relatives, and especially your immediate family, the Scriptures suggest that you are denying your faith and are "worse than an unbeliever."[19]

The purposes of a man's heart are deep waters,
but a man of understanding draws them out.
(Proverbs 20:5)[15]

*And I will ask the Father, and he will give you another
Counselor to be with you forever—the Spirit of truth.*
(John 14:16-17)[16]

But when he, the Spirit of truth, comes,
he will guide you into all truth.
(James 16:13)[17]

Don't have anything to do with foolish and stupid arguments,
because you know they produce quarrels.
(2 Timothy 2:23)[18]

If anyone does not provide for his relatives, and especially
for his immediate family, he has denied the faith
and is worse than an unbeliever.
(1 Timothy 5:8)[19]

Lesson 14

Forgive/Forgiveness

"Forgive and you will be forgiven."
(Luke 6:27)

Forgive: to pardon; to waive any negative feeling or desire for punishment

All of us have been hurt or offended by others at one time or another in our lives. Sometimes these hurts run so deep that it's hard to "let go" of them, even when the person who hurt us has apologized, repented, and asked for forgiveness. When we begin to recognize the depth of our own sin, and the incredible sacrifice that Jesus Christ made on the cross for our sin, we can begin to forgive others, and even ourselves.

Synopsis

We are all sinners.[1] No one is perfect or good except God alone.[2] When God first created the world, it was "good,"[3] but sin soon entered in. It was the mission of Christ to come to this earth to die for our sins so that we might be reconciled with God and have eternal life.[4]

Surely I was sinful at birth, sinful from the time
my mother conceived me.
(Psalm 51:5)[1]

No one is good—except God alone.
(Mark 10:18)[2]

God saw all that he had made, and it was very good.
(Genesis 1:31)[3]

For Christ died for sins once for all, the righteous for
the unrighteous, to bring you to God. He was put
to death in the body but made alive by the Spirit.
(1 Peter 3:18)[4]

When Christ died for us on the cross, He took away all of our sins.[5] Everyone who believes in Jesus Christ, and acknowledges that He died for our sins, receives complete forgiveness of sins.[6] From God's perspective, forgiveness is a "one hundred percent," all-or-none type of thing. That is, when we accept Jesus Christ and repent of our sins, God forgives each and every one of our sins, no matter "how many," "how big," or "how small."

Scriptures give us vivid illustrations of how deep and complete God's forgiveness is for our sins. For example, the Bible states that God: hides our sins behind His back;[7] covers over them;[8] doesn't remember them anymore;[9] removes them "as far as the east is from the west";[10] and, when God forgives us completely we are "whiter than the snow."[11]

God was reconciling the world to himself in Christ,
not counting men's sins against them.
(2 Corinthians 5:19)[5]

Everyone who believes in him receives forgiveness
of sins through his name.
(Acts 10:43)[6]

In your love you kept me from the pit of destruction;
you have put all my sins behind your back.
(Isaiah 38:17)[7]

You forgave the iniquity of your people
and covered all their sins.
(Psalm 85:2)[8]

Their sins and lawless acts
I will remember no more.
(Hebrews 10:17)[9]

As far as the east is from the west,
so far has he removed our transgressions from us.
(Psalm 103:12)[10]

Cleanse me with hyssop, and I will be clean; wash me,
and I will be whiter than snow.
(Psalm 51:7)[11]

God's Guidance

Jesus Christ made it very clear that in order to receive the incredible gift of forgiveness from God, we must first forgive others.[12] There is no "wiggle room." He stated that: *"if you do not forgive men of their sins, your Father will not forgive your sins."*[13]

As human beings, we often find it difficult to forgive the sins of others. Deep down, we would sometimes like to "pick and choose" the sins of others that we will forgive, or decide on "how many" sins the other person has committed against us before they have "exceeded their limit" and we can no longer forgive them. However, Scriptures indicate that God does not allow for this type of "selective" forgiveness when someone repents and asks us for forgiveness.

For example, God's Word makes it clear that when we come to the Lord in prayer, if we hold *"anything* against *anyone,"* we are to forgive him.[14] Along similar lines, we are to forgive *"whatever* grievances you may have against one another."[15]

Forgive and you will be forgiven.
(Luke 6:37)[12]

*For if you forgive men when they sin against you,
your heavenly Father will also forgive you.
But if you do not forgive men their sins,
your Father will not forgive your sins.*
(Matthew 6:14-15)[13]

*And when you stand praying, if you hold anything
against anyone, forgive him, so that your Father
in heaven may forgive you your sins.*
(Mark 11:25)[14]

Bear with each other and forgive whatever grievances
you may have against one another.
Forgive as the Lord forgave you.
(Colossians 3:13)[15]

In addition, if someone genuinely and sincerely repents of his sin, we are to repeatedly forgive him, no matter how many times he repeats the sin, and regardless of how many times he returns to ask for forgiveness.[16]

Finally, in addition to forgiving others, we need to forgive ourselves. When you believe in Jesus Christ, and repent of your sins, you are now blameless before God. Try to fully embrace this fact. Obviously, if the Son of God sets you free from sin, you are free indeed![17]

Then Peter came to Jesus and asked, "Lord, how many times shall I forgive my brother when he sins against me? Up to seven times?" Jesus answered, *"I tell you, not seven times, but seventy-seven times."*
(Matthew 18:21-22)[16]

So if the Son sets you free, you will be free indeed.
(John 8:36)[17]

Lesson 15

Grief

"He heals the brokenhearted and binds
up their wounds."
(Psalm 147:3)

Grief: deep mental suffering, as that arising
from bereavement

Grief is a natural human emotion that is experienced when a significant loss occurs—especially the loss of a loved one. Grief is not necessarily an indication of a lack of faith, but can be an expression of the depth of love we had for someone.

Synopsis

Being a Christian does not rescue us from the pain of loss. Jesus Himself was familiar with grief, and wept when His friend Lazarus died because of His great love for him.[1]

The Bible clearly "makes room" for grief in the hearts of man; there is a time to grieve and a time to mourn.[2] The disciples of Jesus ex-

---

"Where have you laid him?" he asked. *"Come and see, Lord,"*
they replied. Jesus wept. Then the Jews said,
"See how he loved him!"
(John 11:34-36)[1]

There is a time for everything, and a season for every
activity under heaven: a time to be born and a time
to die...a time to weep and a time to laugh...
a time to mourn and a time to dance...
(Ecclesiastes 3:1-2,4)[2]

*"The Son of Man is going to be betrayed into the hands of men.
They will kill him, and on the third day he will be raised to life."*
And the disciples were filled with grief.
(Matthew 17:23)[3]

perienced grief when He told them He was going to die.[3,4] They also mourned immediately after His death on the cross.[5] However, Jesus also told His disciples that their grief would eventually turn to joy when He returned to be with them.[6,7]

As Christians, we will all experience grief when our loved ones die; but we are to maintain a sense of hope, even in the midst of our grief and sorrow.[8] Remember, our grief in this world is only temporary,[9] it will not extend into eternity.[10,11]

Now I am going to him who sent me, yet none of you asks me, "Where are you going?" Because I have said these things, you are filled with grief.
(John 16:5-6)[4]

She went and told those who had been with him and who were mourning and weeping.
(Mark 16:10)[5]

So with you: Now is your time of grief, but I will see you again and you will rejoice, and no one will take away your joy.
(John 16:22)[6]

I tell you the truth, you will weep and mourn while the world rejoices. You will grieve, but your grief will turn to joy.
(John 16:20)[7]

Brothers, we do not want you to be ignorant about those who fall asleep, or to grieve like the rest of men, who have no hope. We believe that Jesus died and rose again and so we believe that God will bring with Jesus those who have fallen asleep in him.
(1 Thessalonians 4:13-14)[8]

In this you greatly rejoice, though now for a little while you may have had to suffer grief in all kinds of trials.
(1 Peter 1:6)[9]

He will wipe every tear from their eyes. There will be no more death or mourning or crying or pain, for the old order of things has passed away.
(Revelation 21:4)[10]

Blessed are you who weep now, for you will laugh.
(Luke 6:21)[11]

Our hope comes from the fact that Jesus Christ defeated death.[12,13] Nothing will ever replace the loss of our loved ones on this earth, but nothing will ever surpass our reunion with them in heaven as we spend eternity with our Lord and Savior Jesus Christ.[14]

If you are grieving and brokenhearted, keep turning to God.[15] Let God help wipe away your tears and heal you wounds.[16,17] He promises He will be close to the brokenhearted and save those who are crushed in spirit.[18]

The last enemy to be destroyed is death.
(1 Corinthians 15:26)[12]

When the perishable has been clothed with the imperishable, and the mortal with immortality, then the saying that is written will come true: "Death has been swallowed up in victory."
(1 Corinthians 15:54)[13]

They will enter into Zion with singing; everlasting joy will crown their heads. Gladness and joy will overtake them, and sorrow and sighing will flee away.
(Isaiah 35:10)[14]

The Spirit helps us in our weakness. We do not know what we ought to pray for, but the Spirit himself intercedes for us with groans that words cannot express.
(Romans 8:26)[15]

The Sovereign LORD will wipe away the tears from all faces.
(Isaiah 25:8)[16]

He heals the brokenhearted and binds up their wounds.
(Psalm 147:3)[17]

The LORD is close to the brokenhearted and saves those who are crushed in spirit.
(Psalm 34:18)[18]

If you know someone who is grieving or mourning, reach out to him or her in Christian love.[19,20] As Christians, we are to carry each other's burdens.[21]

> Rejoice with those who rejoice;
> mourn with those who mourn.
> **(Romans 12:15)**[19]
>
> *By this all men will know that you are my disciples,*
> *if you love one another.*
> **(John 13:35)**[20]
>
> Carry each other's burdens, and in this way
> you will fulfill the law of Christ.
> **(Galatians 6:2)**[21]

Lesson 16

Judgmental

"Do not judge, and you will not be judged."
(Luke 6:37)

*"Rebuke a discerning man, and he
will gain knowledge."*
(Proverbs 19:25)

Judgmental: inclined to pass judgment or condemn
Rebuke: to convey one's disapproval of; reprove

Christians must exercise great care and discernment when judging the actions of other human beings. We must be especially careful not to condemn others or be hypocritical. We must keep in mind that we ourselves are not perfect, and have our own sin with which to contend. However, this does not mean that Christians should avoid judging the actions of others altogether. It is our Christian obligation to rebuke others who are caught in sin so that they may repent and restore their relationship with God.

Synopsis

Jesus preached that human beings should exercise caution and restraint when judging others.[1,2] He emphasized that we should not judge (that is, condemn) others when we ourselves are engag-

---

*Do not judge, and you will not be judged. Do not condemn,
and you will not be condemned.*
(Luke 6:37)[1]

*Do not judge, or you too will be judged. For in the same
way you judge others, you will be judged, and with
the measure you use, it will be measured to you.*
(Matthew 7:1-2)[2]

ing in the same or even "greater" sins.[3] Such actions would be hypocritical.[4]

Similar cautions about judging others are given elsewhere in the Bible. For example, if we pass judgment on others when we ourselves are engaging in the same sin, we bring condemnation upon ourselves,[5] and we will not escape God's judgment.[6]

God is the only true judge of mankind.[7,8] On the final day of judgment, it is God to whom we will have to give an account of our

---

> *Why do you look at the speck of sawdust in your brother's eye and pay no attention to the plank in your own eye? How can you say to your brother, "Let me take the speck out of your eye," when all the time there is a plank in your own eye?*
> **(Matthew 7:3-4)[3]**

> *You hypocrite, first take the plank out of your own eye, and then you will see clearly to remove the speck from your brother's eye.*
> **(Matthew 7:5)[4]**

> You, therefore, have no excuse, you who pass judgment on someone else, for at whatever point you judge the other, you are condemning yourself, because you who pass judgment do the same things.
> **(Romans 2:1)[5]**

> So when you, a mere man, pass judgment on them and yet do the same things, do you think you will escape God's judgment?
> **(Romans 2:3)[6]**

> There is only one Lawgiver and Judge, the one who is able to save and destroy.
> **(James 4:12)[7]**

> It is the Lord who judges me. Therefore, judge nothing before the appointed time; wait till the Lord comes.
> **(1 Corinthians 4:4-5)[8]**

lives—not man.[9] We should seek to be ready for the day of God's judgment. For Christians, this will be a day when we are judged in terms of the rewards we will receive in heaven.[10,11]

God's Guidance

Despite biblical warnings against judging others—especially hypocritical judgment—it is clear from the Scriptures that we should rebuke our fellow Christians when they are caught in sin and are breaking God's moral laws.[12] Such rebuke is important to help restore the person to righteousness, and is a way of showing love for the sinner.[13] In the end, rebuking a sinner from the error of his ways can save his life.[14]

The Bible does not contain any standard "formula" for rebuking others. In some instances the Scriptures recommend that rebuke

---

So then, each of us will give an account of himself to God. Therefore let us stop passing judgment on one another.
(Romans 14:12-13)[9]

Therefore, there is now no condemnation for those who are in Christ Jesus.
(Romans 8:1)[10]

Behold I am coming soon! My reward is with me, and I will give to everyone according to what he has done.
(Revelation 22:12)[11]

So watch yourselves. "If your brother sins, rebuke him, and if he repents, forgive him.
(Luke 17:3)[12]

Those whom I love I rebuke and discipline. So be earnest, and repent.
(Revelation 3:19)[13]

My brothers, if one of you should wander from the truth and someone should bring him back, remember this: Whoever turns a sinner from the error of his way will save him from death and cover over a multitude of sins.
(James 5:19-20)[14]

should be frank,[15] but gentle.[16] Elsewhere, it recommends that rebuke should be public, so that it serves as a warning to others.[17] Finally, the Bible recommends that when we rebuke someone, we use great patience and care.[18]

Perhaps the most effective way of rebuking another person is to simply "speak the truth in love."[19] Humbly point the sinner to God's commandments and the truth as contained in the Holy Scriptures; the Word of God was designed for such purposes.[20]

In the final analysis, rebuke is not something to be avoided, but embraced. If a fellow Christian rebukes you, consider yourself fortunate.[21] You would be wise to listen to rebuke and learn as much

---

Rebuke your neighbor frankly
so you will not share in his guilt.
(Leviticus 19:17)[15]

Brothers, if someone is caught in a sin,
you who are spiritual should restore him gently.
But watch yourself, or you also may be tempted.
(Galatians 6:1)[16]

Those who sin are to be rebuked publicly,
so that the others may take warning.
(1 Timothy 5:20)[17]

Preach the Word; be prepared in season and out of season;
correct, rebuke and encourage—with great patience
and careful instruction.
(2 Timothy 4:2)[18]

Instead, speaking the truth in love, we will in all things
grow up into him who is the Head, that is, Christ.
(Ephesians 4:15)[19]

All Scripture is God-breathed and is useful for teaching,
rebuking, correcting and training in righteousness.
(2 Timothy 3:16)[20]

Like an earring of gold or an ornament of fine gold
is a wise man's rebuke to a listening ear.
(Proverbs 25:12)[21]

as you can from it.[22-24] After all, your response to rebuke may have consequences for eternity.[14]

> He who listens to a life-giving rebuke
> will be at home among the wise.
> **(Proverbs 15:31)**[22]
>
> Rebuke a discerning man,
> and he will gain knowledge.
> **(Proverbs 19:25)**[23]
>
> Whoever gives heed to instruction prospers,
> and blessed is he who trusts in the Lord.
> **(Proverbs 16:20)**[24]

Lesson 17

LOVE

"Give thanks to the Lord, for he is good.
His love endures forever."
(Psalm 136:1)

Love: God is love

The Bible is a love story. It tells of God's unfailing love for mankind. Despite man's shortcomings, God loves each and every one of us and He wants us to love Him. He demonstrated His love for us by sending His only Son as a living sacrifice for our sins. In order to be reconciled with God (and to be restored to a full relationship with Him), all we need to do is to repent of our sins and believe in Christ and the One who sent Him. As Christians, we show our love for Christ by obeying His commands, and passing on God's love and Christ's love to our fellow man.

In order to be truly mentally healthy, you must seek God, discover how much He loves you, fall in love with His Son, Jesus Christ, who died for you, confess your sins, and love one another.

Synopsis

God is love.[1] He is the source of all love.[2] We are able to love because God first loved us.[3] He is loving toward all He has made.[4] It

---

God is love.
(1 John 4:16)[1]

Love comes from God.
(1 John 4:10)[2]

We love because he
first loved us.
(1 John 4:19)[3]

The Lord is faithful to all his
promises and loving toward
all he has made.
(Psalm 145:13)[4]

is difficult to grasp how great and how vast God's love is for us.[5] His love is unfailing,[6] priceless,[6] and everlasting.[7,8]

Because God's nature is love, He commands that we love Him; we are to love God with all our heart, soul, mind, and strength.[9] This is the first and greatest commandment.[10]

If we love God, He promises to watch over us, love us, and protect us.[11,12] God loves those who love Him;[13] if we seek after Him, He promises that we will find Him.[13] If our lives give evidence of love,

> For great is your love, reaching to the heavens;
> your faithfulness reaches to the skies.
> **(Psalm 57:10)**[5]
>
> How priceless is your unfailing love!
> **(Psalm 36:7)**[6]
>
> I [the LORD] have loved you with an
> everlasting love.
> **(Jeremiah 31:3)**[7]
>
> Give thanks to the LORD, for he is good;
> his love endures forever.
> **(1 Chronicles 16:34)**[8]
>
> Love the LORD your God with all your heart and
> with all your soul and with all your strength.
> **(Deuteronomy 6:5)**[9]
>
> "Teacher, which is the greatest commandment in the Law?"
> Jesus replied: " *'Love the Lord your God with all your
> heart and with all your soul and with all your mind.'*"
> **(Matthew 22:36-37)**[10]
>
> The LORD watches over all who love him,
> but all the wicked he will destroy.
> **(Psalm 145:20)**[11]
>
> Spread your protection over them, that those who love
> your name may rejoice in you.
> **(Psalm 5:11)**[12]
>
> I love those who love me,
> and those who seek me find me.
> **(Proverbs 8:17)**[13]

then this is proof that we know God.[14] However, if our lives do not show love, then this is evidence that we do not know God.[15]

God demonstrated His unsurpassing love for mankind by sending His only Son, Jesus Christ, to die for our sins.[16,17] In turn, Christ showed his love for mankind by being obedient to God's will and accepting death on a cross—even though He was innocent and committed no sin.[18] This outpouring of love is further completed when we, in turn, show our love for God by loving Jesus[19] and following His commands.[20,21]

Given God's emphasis on love, it is not surprising that Jesus proclaimed that the second greatest commandment ever given was to

---

Everyone who loves has been born of God
and knows God.
(1 John 4:7)[14]

Whoever does not love does not know God,
because God is love.
(1 John 4:8)[15]

This is love: not that we loved God, but that he loved us and
sent his Son as an atoning sacrifice for our sins.
(1 John 4:10)[16]

*For God so loved the world that he gave his one and only Son,
that whoever believes in him shall not perish but have eternal life.*
(John 3:16)[17]

He suffered death, so that by the grace of God
he might taste death for everyone.
(Hebrews 2:9)[18]

*He who loves me [Jesus] will be loved by my Father,
and I too will love him and show myself to him.*
(John 14:21)[19]

If you love me [Jesus] you will obey what I command.
(John 14:15)[20]

*Whoever has my commands and obeys them,
he is the one who loves me.*
(John 14:21)[21]

"love your neighbor as yourself."[22] This means that Christ wants us to love one another, just as He loved us.[23] In the same manner, we are to treat others just as we would like to be treated.[24]

Our love for others is to be genuine; we are to love one another "deeply, from the heart."[25] When we do this, it is evidence that God lives in us and His love has been made complete in us.[26]

People will know that we are Christ's disciples when we show love to one another.[27] We show our love for Jesus by serving others.[28] If we say that we love God but hate our fellow man, then the Bible says we are liars.[29] Anyone who does not love his brother, whom

---

The second [greatest commandment] is this:
"Love your neighbor as yourself."
There is no commandment greater than these.
(Mark 12:31)[22]

My command is this: Love each other as I have loved you.
(John 15:12)[23]

So in everything, do to others what you would have them do to you, for this sums up the Law of the Prophets.
(Matthew 7:12)[24]

Love one another deeply, from the heart.
(1 Peter 1:22)[25]

No one has ever seen God; but if we love one another, God lives in us and his love is made complete in us.
(1 John 4:12)[26]

By this all men will know that you are my disciples, if you love one another.
(John 13:35)[27]

Again Jesus said, *"Simon son of John, do you truly love me?"* He answered, "Yes, Lord, you know that I love you." Jesus said, *"Take care of my sheep."*
(John 21:16)[28]

If anyone says, "I love God," yet hates his brother, he is a liar. For anyone who does not love his brother, whom he has seen, cannot love God, whom he has not seen.
(1 John 4:20)[29]

he has seen, cannot love God, whom he has not seen.[29] Therefore, God gives us this command: whoever loves God must also love his brother.[30]

Our love for others is not to be limited to the people who "love us back." We are to love everyone, including our enemies and those who persecute us.[31]

Although we are to love all people, our love for others (including our parents or our children) should never surpass our love of Christ.[32] Moreover, our love for money should never be greater than our love for God.[33]

Above all, the greatest expression of our love for others would be to lay down our life for our friends.[34] This is exactly what Jesus did for all of mankind.[35]

And he has given us this command:
Whoever loves God must also love his brother.
(1 John 4:21)[30]

You have heard that it was said, "Love your neighbor and hate your enemy." But I tell you: Love your enemies and pray for those who persecute you, that you may be sons of your Father in heaven.
(Matthew 5:43)[31]

Anyone who loves his father or mother more than me is not worthy of me; anyone who loves his son or daughter more than me is not worthy of me; and anyone who does not take his cross and follow me is not worthy of me.
(Matthew 10:37-38)[32]

No one can serve two masters. Either he will hate the one and love the other, or he will be devoted to the one and despise the other. You cannot serve both God and Money.
(Matthew 6:24)[33]

*Greater love has no one than this,
that he lay down his life for his friends.*
(John 15:13)[34]

I am the good shepherd. The good shepherd lays down his life for the sheep.
(John 10:11)[35]

In the final analysis, the Bible tells us that the only thing that really counts in this life is faith expressing itself through love.[37] No matter what, we are never to let go of love and faith; we are to write them on the "tablets of our hearts."[38] We are to be imitators of God and live a life of love.[39] We are to remain in Christ's love until he returns again to take us into paradise and eternal life.[40,41]

God's Guidance

God has commanded us to love one another, but how do we do this? The best description of love ever given is that written by the apostle Paul in his letter to the church at Corinth. As Christians, we should use these characteristics as a recipe for loving others.

Paul's Description of Love
(Based on: 1 Corinthians 13:4-8)

- **Love is patient.** Be patient with everyone,[42] bearing with one another in love.[43] A man's wisdom[44] and understanding[45] give him patience.

The only thing that counts
is faith expressing itself through love.
(Galatians 5:6)[37]

Let love and faithfulness never leave you; bind them around
your neck, write them on the tablet of your heart.
(Proverbs 3:3)[38]

Be imitators of God, therefore, dearly loved children and
live a life of love, just as Christ loved us and gave himself
up for us as a fragrant offering and sacrifice to God.
(Ephesians 5:1-2)[39]

*As the Father has loved me, so have I loved you.
Now remain in my love.*
(John 15:9)[40]

Keep yourself in God's love as you wait for the mercy of our Lord
Jesus Christ to bring you to eternal life.
(Jude 1:21)[41]

- **Love is kind.** Shower each other with kindness and compassion.[46] Be warmhearted, considerate, and sympathetic. Kindness is one of the "fruits of the Spirit" and evidence that we are Spirit-filled.[47]

- **Love does not envy.** Don't be jealous or envious of the blessings bestowed on other people,[48,49] or envious of other people's skills or talents.[50] A heart at peace gives life, but envy "rots the bones."[51]

And we urge you, brothers, warn those who are idle,
encourage the timid, help the weak, be patient with everyone.
(1 Thessalonians 5:14)[42]

Be patient, bearing with one another in love.
(Ephesians 4:2)[43]

A man's wisdom gives him patience;
it is to his glory to overlook an offense.
(Proverbs 19:11)[44]

A patient man has great understanding,
but a quick-tempered man displays folly.
(Proverbs 14:29)[45]

Be kind and compassionate to one another,
forgiving each other, just as in Christ God forgave you.
(Ephesians 4:32)[46]

But the fruit of the Spirit is love, joy, peace, patience,
kindness, goodness, faithfulness, gentleness and self-control.
(Galatians 5:22-23)[47]

You shall not set your desire on your neighbor's house or land,
his manservant or maidservant, his ox or donkey,
or anything that belongs to your neighbor.
(Deuteronomy 5:21)[48]

Do not be overawed when a man grows rich, when the splendor
of his house increases; for he will take nothing with him
when he dies, his splendor will not descend with him.
(Psalm 49:16-17)[49]

Therefore, rid yourselves of all malice and all deceit,
hypocrisy, envy, and slander of every kind.
(1 Peter 2:1)[50]

A heart at peace gives life to the body, but envy rots the bones.
(Proverbs 14:30)[51]

- **Love does not boast.** Don't brag or boast about yourself to others. All such behavior is evil and does not encourage love.[52] Boast only about the Lord[53] and what He has done for you.[54]

- **Love is not proud.** Pride only breeds quarrels.[55] The Lord detests the proud of heart.[56] Honor one another above yourself[57,58] and clothe yourself with humility.[59]

- **Love is not rude.** Try to be polite, courteous, considerate,[60,61] and well-mannered. Don't be rude or crude. Let your gentleness be evident to all.[62]

You boast and brag. All such boasting is evil.
(James 4:16)[52]

Let him who boasts boast in the Lord.
(1 Corinthians 1:31)[53]

May I never boast except in the cross
of our Lord Jesus Christ.
(Galatians 6:14)[54]

Pride only breeds quarrels; but wisdom is found
in those who take advice.
(Proverbs 13:10)[55]

The LORD detests all the proud of heart. Be sure of this:
They will not go unpunished.
(Proverbs 16:5)[56]

Honor one another above yourselves.
(Romans 12:10)[57]

Do nothing out of selfish ambition or vain conceit,
but in humility consider others better than yourselves.
(Philippians 2:3)[58]

All of you, clothe yourselves with humility toward one another.
(1 Peter 5:5)[59]

But the wisdom that comes from heaven is first of all pure;
then peace-loving, considerate, submissive, full of mercy
and good fruit, impartial and sincere.
(James 3:17)[60]

- **Love is not self-seeking.** Don't focus on what you can get out of the relationship (what's in it for you), but focus on what you can *give* to the relationship. Self-seeking people can provoke God's wrath and anger.[63]

- **Love is not easily angered.** Try to stay calm, and don't be quickly provoked into anger.[64] Anger stirs up disagreements and fights, and a hot-tempered man commits many sins.[65] Make every effort to live at peace with everyone.[66]

- **Love keeps no record of wrongs.** Don't keep bringing up past hurts or offenses. Forgive one another, just as in Christ, God forgave you.[67] No matter how many times you are hurt, if the person repents, keep on forgiving.[68]

Husbands, in the same way be considerate as you live with
your wives, and treat them with respect as the weaker partner
and as heirs with you of the gracious gift of life,
so that nothing will hinder your prayers.
(1 Peter 3:7)[61]

Let your gentleness be evident to all.
(Philippians 4:5)[62]

But for those who are self-seeking and who reject the truth
and follow evil, there will be wrath and anger.
(Romans 2:8)[63]

Do not be quickly provoked in your spirit,
for anger resides in the lap of fools.
(Ecclesiastes 7:9)[64]

An angry man stirs up dissension,
and a hot-tempered one commits many sins.
(Proverbs 29:22)[65]

Make every effort to live in peace with all men and to be holy.
(Hebrews 12:14)[66]

Bear with each other and forgive whatever grievances you may
have against one another. Forgive as the Lord forgave you.
(Colossians 3:13)[67]

Then Peter came to Jesus and asked, "Lord, how many times shall I forgive my brother when he sins against me? Up to seven times?" Jesus answered, *I tell you, not seven times, but seventy-seven times.*
(Matthew 18:21-22)[68]

- **Love does not delight in evil.** Don't take delight in hurting others, or being mean or abusive, or otherwise sinful. Turn from evil and do good instead.[69]

- **Love rejoices in the truth.** Don't tell lies[70] or deceive.[71] God detests those who tell lies, but delights in those who are truthful.[72]

- **Love always protects.** Protect others from harm and keep them safe, just as God protects those He loves.[73,74] He is a shield for all who take refuge in Him.[75] Show your love for others by protecting them from harm.

- **Love always trusts.** Build trust in your relationships. Keep your word. Follow through. Be loving. Be reasonable and predictable. Don't lose control or be abusive or aggressive. Trust in God and do good.[76]

Turn from evil and do good;
then you will dwell in the land forever.
(Psalm 37:27)[69]

Keep falsehood and lies far from me.
(Proverbs 30:8)[70]

Do not lie. Do not deceive one another.
(Leviticus 19:11)[71]

The LORD detests lying lips,
but he delights in men who are truthful.
(Proverbs 12:22)[72]

The LORD is my strength and my shield;
my heart trusts in him, and I am helped.
(Psalm 28:7)[73]

"Because of the oppression of the weak and the groaning
of the needy, I will now arise," says the LORD.
"I will protect them from those who malign them."
(Psalm 12:5)[74]

He is a shield for all who take refuge in him.
(Psalm 18:30)[75]

Trust in the LORD and do good.
(Psalm 37:3)[76]

- **Love always hopes.** Don't give up hope, no matter what difficulties you may be having in your relationship.[77] Keep positive and optimistic.[78] God is a God of miracles; nothing is impossible with God.[79] If you feel hopeless, try putting your hope in God.[80]

- **Love always perseveres.** Be persistent in your love for others. Don't give up on them or be discouraged.

- **Love never fails.** Even though you may experience difficulties along the road, loving another person always succeeds in the end. Your efforts will always bear fruit. Do everything in love.[81]

As we set about loving one another, rest assured that no matter what happens in life, those who believe in God will never be alone and will never be separated from God's love. The apostle Paul etched these sentiments into the history of mankind with these incredible words of assurance from Romans 8:38-39:

"For I am convinced that neither death nor life, neither angels nor demons, neither the present nor the future, nor any powers, neither height nor depth, nor anything else in all creation, will be able to separate us from the love of God that is in Christ Jesus our Lord."

Anyone who is among the living has hope.
(Ecclesiastes 9:4)[77]

Finally, brothers, whatever is true, whatever is noble, whatever is right, whatever is pure, whatever is lovely, whatever is admirable—if anything is excellent or praiseworthy—think about such things.
(Philippians 4:8)[78]

For nothing is impossible with God.
(Luke 1:37)[79]

Find rest, O my soul, in God alone; my hope comes from him.
(Psalm 62:5)[80]

Do everything in love.
(1 Corinthians 16:14)[81]

Lesson 18

Marriage

"For this reason a man will leave his father and mother and be united to his wife, and the two will become one flesh."
(Mark 10:7-8)

Marriage: the legal union of two people of the opposite sex as husband and wife

Marriage is a sacred institution that God established from the beginning of mankind. If you are married or plan to be married, turn to the Scriptures for important advice and guidance.

Synopsis

The institution of marriage can be traced to the creation story. After God created Adam, He realized it was not good for man to be alone and so He decided to make a helpmate for him,[1] and so He created Eve, the first woman. It was precisely at this point in time—after God created "woman"— that the first reference to marriage appears in the Scriptures. God announced that the desire for "woman" would be for her "*husband*," and that her husband would rule over her.[2] The use of the term "husband" represents the first reference in the Bible to the institution of marriage.

The LORD God said, "It is not good for the man to be alone. I will make a helper suitable for him."
(Genesis 2:18)[1]

Your desire will be for your husband,
and he will rule over you.
(Genesis 3:16)[2]

Subsequent Scriptures lend further support to the fact that it is God's general plan for men and women to be married—for children to grow up, leave their mothers and fathers, be united in marriage, and become one flesh.[3]

However, this is not to say that *all* men and women, without exception, must get married. For example, Jesus acknowledged that some people might properly renounce marriage because of physical limitations or because of their focus on the kingdom of heaven.[4]

The apostle Paul went even further; he advocated staying single for life (like he was) if at all possible. However, he recommended that men and women who could not control themselves should get married so that they didn't "burn with passion" or fall prey to sexual immorality.[5,6]

Finally, Paul made another noteworthy recommendation regarding marriage. He urged that if you are a believer in Jesus Christ you should never marry anyone who is an unbeliever.[7]

For this reason a man will leave his father and mother and be united to his wife, and the two will become one flesh.
(Mark 10:7-8)[3]

For some are eunuchs because they were born that way; others were made that way by men; and others have renounced marriage because of the kingdom of heaven. The one who can accept this should accept it.
(Matthew 19:12)[4]

Now to the unmarried and widows I say: It is good for them to stay unmarried, as I am. But if they cannot control themselves, they should marry, for it is better to marry than to burn with passion.
(1 Corinthians 7:8-9)[5]

It is good for man not to marry. But since there is so much immorality, each man should have his own wife, and each woman her own husband.
(1 Corinthians 7:1-2)[6]

Do not be yoked together with unbelievers.
(2 Corinthians 6:14)[7]

God's Guidance

Husbands

Men, if you are blessed by finding a wife, you should be thankful. The Bible proclaims that he who has found a wife has found "what is good" and will receive favor from the Lord.[8] You are to love your wife and sacrifice for her just as Christ loved the church and gave Himself up for her to make her holy.[9] You are to provide for your wife and take care of her, just as you love your own body and take care of it.[10] You are to be considerate and treat her with respect, and not be harsh with her.[11]

He who finds a wife finds what is good and
receives favor from the LORD.
(Proverbs 18:22)[8]

Husbands, love your wives, just as Christ loved the
church and gave himself up for her to make her holy.
(Ephesians 5:25-26)[9]

Husbands ought to love their wives as their own bodies.
He who loves his wife loves himself. After all, no one
ever hated his own body, but he feeds and cares for it,
just as Christ does the church.
(Ephesians 5:28-29)[10]

Husbands, in the same way be considerate as you
live with your wives, and treat them with respect
as the weaker partner and as heirs with you of the
gracious gift of life, so that nothing will
hinder your prayers.
(1 Peter 3:7)[11]

Now as the church submits to Christ,
so also wives should submit to their husbands in everything.
(Ephesians 5:24)[12]

Now I want you to realize that the head of every man is Christ,
and the head of the woman is man, and the head of Christ is God.
(1 Corinthians 11:3)[13]

Wives, submit to your husbands as to the Lord.
(Ephesians 5:22)[14]

Wives

Women, you were created to be a helpmate[1] for your husband and you are to submit to him in everything.[12] This may sound like a difficult task, but the Scriptures indicate that if your husband is properly submissive to Jesus Christ, you can submit to him with confidence. Since God is the head of Jesus, when you submit to your husband it is the same thing as submitting to the Lord.[13,14]

Wives, you are to dress modestly and not focus on "beauty" and outward adornment; instead, you should focus on your "inner self" and possess the unfading beauty of a gentle and quiet spirit, "which is of great worth in God's sight."[15] You should be clothed with "strength and dignity" and take care of your household and not be lazy.[16] You should possess a noble character,[17] refrain from malicious talk,[18] be prudent (exercise good judgment and common sense),[19] be trustworthy in everything,[18] and speak with wisdom and faithful instruction.[16]

> Your beauty should not come from outward adornment,
> such as braided hair and the wearing of gold jewelry
> and fine clothes. Instead, it should be that of your inner self,
> the unfading beauty of a gentle and quiet spirit,
> which is of great worth in God's sight.
> **(1 Peter 3:3-4)**[15]
>
> She is clothed with strength and dignity; she can laugh
> at the days to come. She speaks with wisdom,
> and faithful instruction is on her tongue.
> She watches over the affairs of her household
> and does not eat of the bread of idleness.
> **(Proverbs 31:25-27)**[16]
>
> A wife of noble character is her husband's crown,
> but a disgraceful wife is like decay in his bones.
> **(Proverbs 12:4)**[17]
>
> In the same way, their wives are to be women worthy
> of respect, not malicious talkers but temperate and
> trustworthy in everything.
> **(1 Timothy 3:11)**[18]
>
> Houses and wealth are inherited from parents,
> but a prudent wife is from the LORD.
> **(Proverbs 19:14)**[19]

Lesson 19

Money/Riches

"Keep your lives free from the love of money and
be content with what you have."
(Hebrews 13:5)

Money: the unit of currency used to purchase
or exchange goods or services

Some people love money and spend their whole lives focused on acquiring material things. In the Bible, God repeatedly warns against this approach to life. It is "ok" to have money, as long as money does not have you. Turn to God's Word to find the proper balance and perspective on money and riches.

Synopsis

God warns Christians to keep their lives free from the love of money and to be content with whatever they have.[1] The Scriptures advise that people who run around trying to get rich are often led into foolish and harmful desires, which ultimately plunge them into ruin and destruction.[2] In a curious paradox, God points out that people who love money never seem to have enough[3]—they always seem to want "just a little more."

Keep your lives free from the love of money and be content
with what you have, because God has said,
"Never will I leave you; never will I forsake you."
(Hebrews 13:5)[1]

People who want to get rich fall into temptation and
a trap and into many foolish and harmful desires
that plunge men into ruin and destruction.
(1 Timothy 6:10)[2]

People with money and riches can also develop a false sense of security. They imagine their money to be a "fortified city," and that they are safe behind its walls.[4] However, God can see behind the wall to view our true selves. And when He looks behind the wall at the rich man, He often sees a person who is "wretched, pitiful, poor, blind and naked."[5]

Not only can God see behind the wall, He can also see the ironic folly of building up treasures on earth. After a lifetime of "heaping up wealth," the rich man dies and does not take anything with him after death.[6] He came into the world naked, and he leaves naked.[7]

If you are fortunate enough to accumulate wealth, do not set your heart on it.[8] Keep in mind, that as soon as you start focusing on making money, you can lose everything you have in the blink of an eye.[9]

Whoever loves money never has money enough; whoever loves wealth is never satisfied with his income. This too is meaningless.
(Ecclesiastes 5:10)[3]

The wealth of the rich is their fortified city;
they imagine it an unscalable wall.
(Proverbs 18:11)[4]

You say, "I am rich; I have acquired wealth and do not need a thing." But you do not realize that you are wretched, pitiful, poor, blind and naked.
(Revelation 3:17)[5]

Do not be overawed when a man grows rich, when the splendor of his house increases; for he will take nothing with him when he dies.
(Psalm 49:16-17)[6]

Naked I came from my mother's womb, and naked I will depart.
(Job 1:20)[7]

Though your riches increase, do not set your heart on them.
(Psalm 62:10)[8]

Cast but a glance at riches, and they are gone, for they will surely sprout wings and fly off to the sky like an eagle.
(Proverbs 23:5)[9]

Finally, because of the many dangers associated with money—the temptations, pitfalls, and snares—Jesus Christ reminds us how hard it is for a rich man to get into heaven.[10] By way of illustration, He points out that it would be easier for a camel (a large animal) to go through a little door in the walled city (the so-called "eye of the needle"), than it would be for a rich man to get into heaven.[11]

God's Guidance

Instead of putting our hope in wealth, Scriptures recommend that we put our hope in God.[12] Instead of being rich in terms of money, the Bible recommends that we be rich in good deeds and generosity.[13] Instead of storing up treasures on earth, Jesus Christ recommends that we store up treasures in heaven, where no thief can steal it, and it will not be destroyed.[14] Instead of be-

---

How hard it is for the rich to enter the kingdom of God.
(Mark 10:23)[10]

It is easier for a camel to go through the eye of a needle than for a rich man to enter the kingdom of God.
(Mark 10:25)[11]

Command those who are rich in this present world not to be arrogant nor to put their hope in wealth, which is so uncertain, but to put their hope in God, who richly provides us with everything for our enjoyment.
(1 Timothy 6:17)[12]

Command them to do good, to be rich in good deeds, and to be generous and willing to share. In this way they will lay up treasure for themselves as a firm foundation for the coming age, so that they may take hold of the life that is truly life.
(1 Timothy 6:18-19)[13]

Sell your possessions and give to the poor. Provide purses for yourselves that will not wear out, a treasure in heaven that will not be exhausted, where no thief comes near and no moth destroys.
(Luke 12:33)[14]

ing rich in terms of how much gold and silver we own, it is better to be rich in terms of wisdom and understanding.[15]

Above all else, as Christians we are to seek righteousness rather than wealth.[16] In the words of Jesus Christ: "But seek first the kingdom and his righteousness, and all these things will be given to you as well." [17]

> How much better to get wisdom than gold,
> to choose understanding rather than silver!
> **(Proverbs 16:16)**[15]
>
> Wealth is worthless in the day of wrath,
> but righteousness delivers from death.
> **(Proverbs 11:4)**[16]
>
> *But seek first his kingdom and his righteousness,*
> *and all these things will be given to you as well.*
> **(Matthew 6:33)**[17]

Lesson 20

Parenting

"Train a child in the way he should go, and when
he is old he will not turn from it."
(Proverbs 22:6)

Parenting: the process of raising and educating
a child from birth to adulthood.

Being a parent is not easy in today's society. The media and the secular world are full of advice on how to raise children. Parenting is made even more difficult by divorce, poverty, and violence that are prevalent in our modern world. If you are confused, turn to God's Word for help and guidance.

Synopsis

Above all else, Christian parenting is to be based on love. As you go about the task of raising children, you are to love them deeply from the heart,[1] just as God loves you.[2] In fact, everything you do with your child should be based on love.[3] If you become discouraged in your role as a parent, remember that even if you make "mistakes," love will make up for your lack of perfection.[4] In the final analysis, love never fails.[5]

Love one another deeply,
from the heart.
(1 Peter 1:22)[1]

Dear friends, let us love one another,
for love comes from God.
(1 John 4:7)[2]

Do everything in love.
(1 Corinthians 16:14)[3]

One of the most important ways you can show love to your children is to teach them the Bible. God's Word contains an important reference guide on training your children to behave and act appropriately. Hiding the Scriptures in your child's heart will help him resist sin,[6] and ensure that when he grows up he will not turn from God's commandments.[7]

As you teach your children, try to be positive,[8] and be careful how you talk to them. When you speak, try to be Christ-like,[9] and remember that "reckless words pierce like a sword,"[10] and the things you say to your child in anger can have significant impact on their entire lives. Learn to hold your tongue.[11,12] Be patient and kind;[13,14]

Above all, love each other deeply, because love covers over a multitude of sins. **(1 Peter 4:8)**[4]

Love never fails. **(1 Corinthians 13:8)**[5]

I have hidden your word in my heart that I might not sin against you. **(Psalm 119:11)**[6]

Train a child in the way he should go, and when he is old he will not turn from it. **(Proverbs 22:6)**[7]

Pleasant words promote instruction. **(Proverbs 16:21)**[8]

If anyone speaks, he should do it as one speaking the very words of God. **(1 Peter 4:11)**[9]

Reckless words pierce like a sword, but the tongue of the wise brings healing. **(Proverbs 12:18)**[10]

Set a guard over my mouth, O LORD; keep watch over the door of my lips. **(Psalm 141:3)**[11]

When words are many, sin is not absent, but he who holds his tongue is wise. **(Proverbs 10:19)**[12]

Be patient, bearing with one another in love. **(Ephesians 4:2)**[13]

Love is patient, love is kind. **(1 Corinthians 13:4)**[14]

speak quietly, and try not to shout all the time.[15] Think before you speak,[16] and be careful not to embitter[17] or exasperate[19] your children. Treat all your children equally, and do not show favoritism for one child or the other.[19]

Another way you can show love to your child is through the proper application of discipline.[20] When considering different forms of discipline, the Bible clearly advocates corporal punishment as an essential technique for training children.[21] Of course, there are other forms of discipline that parents can use, and great care must be taken when administering corporal punishment.**

The quiet words of the wise are more to be heeded
than the shouts of a ruler of fools.
(Ephesians 9:17)[15]

Do you see a man who speaks in haste?
There is more hope for a fool than for him.
(Proverbs 29:20)[16]

Fathers, do not embitter your children,
or they will become discouraged.
(Colossians 3:21)[17]

Fathers, do not exasperate your children; instead,
bring them up in the training and instruction of the Lord.
(Ephesians 6:4)[18]

To show partiality in judging is not good.
(Proverbs 24:23)[19]

He who spares the rod hates his son,
but he who loves him is careful to discipline him.
(Proverbs 13:24)[20]

Do not withhold discipline from a child; if you punish
him with the rod, he will not die. Punish him with the rod
and save his soul from death.
(Proverbs 23:13-14)[21]

** **Please Note:** Solomon's advice was to use a "rod" when disciplining. However, in today's society, this form of punishment is generally not permissible under current laws and social norms. Other forms of corporal punishment, such as spanking with your hand, would normally be permissible. If you have any questions, check with your local authorities.

However, based on King Solomon's advice, appropriate use of corporal punishment is clearly consistent with Biblical guidance.[22,23] In fact, properly administered corporal punishment may be important for your child's very salvation.[21]

When you discipline your children (in whatever form), you are giving them a blessing, just as we ourselves are blessed when God disciplines us.[24] God disciplines us for our sin,[25] and this discipline is good for us, so that we may share in His holiness.[26]

When you receive discipline from God, or when you give discipline to your children, it isn't very pleasant, nor is it meant to be.[27] However, the "fruits" of discipline are worth the "pain." Discipline

---

The rod of correction imparts wisdom,
but a child left to himself disgraces his mother.
(Proverbs 29:15)[22]

Folly is bound up in the heart of a child,
but the rod of discipline will drive it far from him.
(Proverbs 22:15)[23]

Blessed is the man whom God corrects; so do not despise the
discipline of the Almighty. For he wounds,
but he also binds up; he injures,
but his hands also heal.
(Job 5:17-18)[24]

You rebuke and discipline men for their sin.
(Psalm 39:11)[25]

Our fathers disciplined us for a little while as
they thought best; but God disciplines for our good,
that we may share in his holiness.
(Hebrews 12:10)[26]

No discipline seems pleasant at the time, but painful.
Later on, however, it produces a harvest of
righteousness and peace for those
who have been trained by it.
(Hebrews 12:11)[27]

makes us wise,[28] helps keep us out of trouble,[29] and helps us lead successful and honorable lives.[30]

Some parents worry that if they discipline their children that their children will not "like them." The main goal of parenting is not to have your children like you; however, it is extremely important that your children grow up to obey you and respect you.[31,32]

Finally, some parents worry that if they discipline their children, their children will be "afraid of them," or fear them; however, a child's fear of his parents is not necessarily a bad thing. A child's fear of his parents is analogous to an adult's fear of God. Proper fear of our heavenly Father[33] helps keep us from sinning,[34] and makes us wiser.[35]

Whoever loves discipline loves knowledge,
but he who hates correction is stupid.
(Proverbs 12:1)[28]

He will die for lack of discipline,
led astray by his own great folly.
(Proverbs 5:23)[29]

He who ignores discipline comes to poverty and shame,
but whoever heeds correction is honored.
(Proverbs 13:18)[30]

He must manage his own family well and see that
his children obey him with proper respect.
(1 Timothy 3:4)[31]

We have all had fathers who disciplined us and we
respected them for it. How much more should we
submit to the Father of our spirits and live!
(Hebrews 12:9)[32]

Fear the LORD your God, serve him only
and take your oaths in his name.
(Deuteronomy 6:13)[33]

Moses said to the people, "Do not be afraid. God has
come to test you, so that the fear of God will be with you
and keep you from sinning."
(Exodus 20:20)[34]

Bottom line...when you properly discipline your children, things will turn out better for *you* and for them. When children are properly disciplined, they tend to live more righteous lives;[27] and when they grow up, they bring peace and joy to their parents.[36]

> The fear of the L‍ord is the beginning of wisdom,
> and knowledge of the Holy One is understanding.
> **(Proverbs 9:10)**[35]
>
> Discipline your son, and he will give you peace;
> he will bring delight to your soul.
> **(Proverbs 29:17)**[36]

A Final Note: Most authorities would not advocate corporal punishment before age 1 or after the age of 8-years-old. To be effective, corporal punishment should be used cautiously and sparingly. It is most often recommended for use in connection with dangerous or clearly defiant behaviors exhibited by the child. Of course, not all modern authorities would agree with the use of corporal punishment. The biblical perspective is emphasized in this Lesson, as found in God's Word.

Lesson 21

Persecution

"If you suffer as a Christian, do not be ashamed, but praise God that you bear that name."
(1 Peter 4:16)

Persecute: to oppress, subjugate, or harass a specific group of people.

Christians are under attack throughout the world. In some countries, they are not permitted to practice their faith. In other countries, Christians are actively persecuted or tortured because of their beliefs, even to the point of death.

Many Christians are surprised or dismayed at the persecution they suffer. However, God's Word tells us that Christians should not expect to live trouble free lives and that they should view persecution as a blessing for those who believe in Jesus Christ and who suffer for their faith.

Synopsis

Modern day persecution of Christians has its origins in the suffering endured by the earliest followers of Christ. Jesus' disciples were hated, rejected, falsely accused, and insulted because of their belief in Him and because they followed His teachings. Christ was sensitive to their pain and took time to comfort them. He told His followers to be glad and rejoice that they were suffering in His name.[1] He called them "blessed" when they were hated, insulted,

---

Blessed are you when people insult you, persecute you and falsely say all kinds of evil against you, because of me. Rejoice and be glad, because great is your reward in heaven.
(Matthew 5:11-12)[1]

and rejected for His sake.[2] He promised them that after they had suffered a little while on this earth, they would be rewarded greatly in heaven.[1,3]

Jesus was familiar with persecution because He Himself suffered at the hands of others throughout His ministry.[4] Because He was hated by many of His contemporaries, He knew that His followers would also be hated.[5,6] In the end, Jesus endured the ultimate persecution when He was unjustly crucified on the cross.[7-9]

Blessed are you when men hate you, when they exclude you and insult you and reject your name as evil, because of the Son of Man.
(Luke 6:22)[2]

All men will hate you because of me, but he who stands firm to the end will be saved.
(Mark 13:13)[3]

He was despised and rejected by men, a man of sorrows, and familiar with suffering.
(Isaiah 53:3)[4]

No servant is greater than his master. If they persecuted me they will persecute you also.
(John 15:20)[5]

If the world hates you, keep in mind that it hated me first.
(John 15:18)[6]

But he was pierced for our transgressions, he was crushed for our iniquities...and by his wounds we are healed.
(Isaiah 53:5)[7]

From that time on Jesus began to explain to his disciples that he must go to Jerusalem and suffer many things at the hands of the elders, chief priests and teachers of the law, and that he must be killed and on the third day be raised to life.
(Matthew 16:21)[8]

They stripped him and put a scarlet robe on him, and then twisted together a crown of thorns and set it on his head. They put a staff in his right hand and knelt in front of him and mocked him. "Hail, king of the Jews!" they said.
(Matthew 27:28-29)[9]

After His crucifixion, Christ's followers and all of the original disciples (except Judas) continued to be persecuted for their faith as they spread the word about Jesus throughout the world.[10,11] Many of the disciples wrote about their suffering and pointed to the "positive" aspects of persecution.

God's Guidance

If you suffer because you are a Christian, do not to be ashamed.[12] If you suffer because you are doing good, this is commendable in the sight of God.[13] Commit yourself to God's work, and keep doing good.[14,15]

> It was about this time that Kind Herod arrested some who belonged to the church, intending to persecute them. He had James, the brother of John, put to death with the sword. When he saw that this pleased the Jews, he proceeded to seize Peter also.
> **(Acts 12:2-3)**[10]

> They [the Jews] stirred up persecution against Paul and Barnabas, and expelled them from the region.
> **(Acts 13:50)**[11]

> If you suffer as a Christian, do not be ashamed, but praise God that you bear that name.
> **(1 Peter 4:16)**[12]

> If you suffer for doing good and you endure it, this is commendable before God.
> **(1 Peter 2:2)**[13]

> So then, those who suffer according to God's will should commit themselves to the faithful Creator and continue to do good.
> **(1 Peter 4:19)**[14]

> It is better, if it is God's will, to suffer for doing good than for doing evil.
> **(1 Peter 3:17)**[15]

If you have been insulted because you are a Christian, consider yourself blessed.[16] You should never fear the fact that men "put you down" or insult you because of your beliefs.[17]

If you are a Christian, you should not be surprised that you are being persecuted.[18,19] If you are living a Godly life in Christ Jesus, you should expect to be persecuted.[20] Remember that Christ was persecuted and suffered for us and left us an example that we should all follow.[21,22]

> If you are insulted because of the name of Christ,
> you are blessed, for the Spirit of glory
> and of God rests on you.
> **(1 Peter 4:14)**[16]

> Do not fear the reproach of men
> or be terrified by their insults.
> **(Isaiah 51:7)**[17]

> Do not be surprised, my brothers,
> if the world hates you.
> **(1 John 3:13)**[18]

> Dear friends, do not be surprised at the painful trial
> you are suffering, as though something strange
> were happening to you.
> **(1 Peter 4:12-13)**[19]

> In fact, everyone who wants to live a godly life in Christ
> Jesus will be persecuted, while evil men and imposters
> will go from bad to worse, deceiving and being deceived.
> **(2 Timothy 3:12-13)**[20]

> Christ suffered for you, leaving you an example,
> that you should follow in his steps.
> **(1 Peter 2:21)**[21]

> For it has been granted to you on behalf of Christ
> not only to believe on him, but also to suffer for him.
> **(Philippians 1:29)**[22]

Finally, despite the fact that Christians are often persecuted for their faith, take comfort in the fact that the Holy Scriptures promise us that nothing (including persecution) will ever separate us from the love of God that is in Christ Jesus our Lord.[23]

> Who shall separate us from the love of Christ? Shall trouble or hardship or persecution or famine or nakedness or danger or sword? As it is written:
>
> "For your sake we face death all day long;
> we are considered as sheep to be slaughtered."
>
> No, in all these things we are more than conquerors through him who loved us. For I am convinced that neither death nor life, neither angels nor demons, neither the present nor the future, nor any powers, neither height nor depth, nor anything else in all creation, will be able to separate us from the love of God that is in Christ Jesus our Lord.
> **(Romans 8:35-39)**[23]

Lesson 22

PRAYER

The "Lord's Prayer"

This, then, is how you should pray:

"Our Father in heaven,
hallowed be your name,
your kingdom come,
your will be done
on earth as it is in heaven.
Give us today our daily bread.
Forgive us our debts,
As we also have forgiven our debtors.
And lead us not into temptation,
But deliver us from the evil one."
(Matthew 6:9-13)

Prayer: a reverent petition made to God

Prayer is a hallmark of the Christian faith. The importance of prayer is emphasized throughout the Bible—from the Old Testament to the New Testament.

Jesus Christ set the example for prayer. He prayed regularly and took time to teach His disciples how to pray.

The essence of prayer is communication, and its main purpose is to develop and maintain a close relationship with God. God's response to our prayers depends less upon what we ask of Him, and more upon the attitude of our heart and its inclination to please God and live according to His will.

Synopsis

The Lord God Almighty, the creator of all things, gives us a personal invitation to pray to Him.[1] We develop our relationship with God by drawing near to Him—humbly and reverently coming into His presence.[2,3] The purpose of prayer is not to change God's mind or convince Him of our needs. God knows our needs before we ask.[4]

Jesus Christ, our Lord and Savior, was well aware of the importance of prayer. Throughout His ministry on earth, Christ set an example of a prayer-filled life and encouraged others to follow His example. As Christians, we should devote our lives to prayer.[5,6]

Prayer is not intended to be something we do only on special occasions—when we are hurting, or when we need something from God. To be sure, praying when we are in trouble,[7] sick,[8] or in need of a

---

This is what the LORD says, he who made the earth, the LORD who formed it and established it—the LORD is his name: "Call to me and I will answer you and tell you great and unsearchable things you do not know."
(Jeremiah 33:2-3)[1]

Come near to God and he will come near to you.
(James 4:8)[2]

It is good to be near to God.
(Psalm 73:28)[3]

For your Father knows what you need before you ask him.
(Matthew 6:8)[4]

Devote yourselves to prayer, being watchful and thankful.
(Colossians 4:2)[5]

Be joyful in hope, patient in affliction, faithful in prayer.
(Romans 12:12)[6]

Is any one of you in trouble? He should pray.
(James 5:13)[7]

And the prayer offered in faith will make the sick person well; the Lord will raise him up.
(James 5:15)[8]

miracle,[9] are completely acceptable reasons to pray. However, prayer should not be limited to any particular topics.

The Bible encourages us to "pray continually" and give thanks in "all circumstances."[10] Jesus told His disciples that they should "always pray and not give up."[11] Ideally, our entire lives (actions, thoughts, and deeds) should be conducted in a prayerful manner—abiding in Christ,[12] doing what is pleasing to Him,[13] and seeking His will.[14]

In addition to encouraging a personal prayer life, the Bible emphasizes the power of corporate prayer—two or more Christians coming together and praying for a common cause.[15,16] The members of

---

O LORD my God, I called to you for help and you healed me.
(Psalm 30:2)[9]

Be joyful always; pray continually; give thanks in all circumstances, for this is God's will for you in Christ Jesus.
(1 Thessalonians 5:16-18)[10]

Then Jesus told His disciples a parable to show them that they should always pray and not give up.
(Luke 18:1)[11]

If you remain in me and my words remain in you, ask whatever you wish, and it will be given to you.
(John 15:7)[12]

Dear friends, if our hearts do not condemn us, we have confidence before God and receive from him anything we ask, because we obey his commands and do what pleases him.
(1 John 3:21-22)[13]

This is the confidence we have in approaching God: that if we ask anything according to his will, he hears us.
(1 John 5:14)[14]

Again, I tell you that if two of you on earth agree about anything you ask for, it will be done for you by my Father in heaven. For where two or three come together in my name, there am I with them.
(Matthew 18:19-20)[15]

They all joined together constantly in prayer, along with the women and Mary the mother of Jesus, and with his brothers.
(Acts 1:12)[16]

the early church recognized the importance of communal prayer; they devoted themselves to the apostles' teaching, to fellowship, to the breaking of bread, and to prayer.[17]

As mentioned earlier, there is no exclusive or preferred topic of prayer; the Bible encourages us to pray for everything and for everyone, including ourselves.[18-20] Because of the limitless possibilities for prayer, it is perhaps not surprising that the disciples of Jesus Christ asked Him to teach them how to pray.[21] In response to this request, Jesus provided the "model" prayer for Christians, which has come to be called the "Lord's Prayer."

> They devoted themselves to the apostles' teaching and to the fellowship, to the breaking of bread and to prayer.
> **(Acts 2:42)**[17]
>
> Do not be anxious about anything, but in everything, by prayer and petition, with thanksgiving, present your requests to God.
> **(Philippians 4:6)**[18]
>
> I urge, then, first of all, that requests, prayers, intercession and thanksgiving be made for everyone—for kings and all those in authority, that we may live peaceful and quiet lives in all godliness and holiness.
> **(1 Timothy 2:1-2)**[19]
>
> And pray in the Spirit on all occasions with all kinds of prayers and requests. With this in mind, be alert and always keep on praying for all the saints.
> **(Ephesians 6:18)**[20]
>
> One day Jesus was praying in a certain place. When he finished, one of his disciples said to him, "Lord, teach us to pray, just as John taught his disciples."
> **(Luke 11:1)**[21]

"I pray because I can't help myself. I pray because I'm helpless. I pray because the need flows out of me all the time—waking and sleeping. It doesn't change God—it changes me."
- **C. S. Lewis**

The "Lord's Prayer"

The Lord's Prayer (see p. 151) highlights five major topics for prayer.

1. **Praise and Worship:**[22] We pray to give thanks to God,[23] to praise Him,[24] and to glorify His name.[25]

2. **Submission to God's Will:** We pray for God's will to be done on earth as it is in heaven.[26] The mission of Jesus was to do the will of His Father.[27] We also are to submit our will to God's will.[28]

<u>Our Father in heaven, hallowed be your name.</u>
(Matthew 6:9)[22]

Give thanks to the LORD, for he is good.
His love endures forever.
(Psalm 136:1)[23]

Praise the LORD, O my soul; all my inmost being,
praise his holy name.
(Psalm 103:1)[24]

I will glorify your name forever.
(Psalm 86:12)[25]

<u>Your kingdom come,
your will be done on earth as it is in heaven.</u>
(Matthew 6:10)[26]

*For I have come down from heaven not to do my will
but to do the will of him who sent me.*
(John 6:38)[27]

Submit yourselves, then, to God.
(James 4:7)[28]

3. **Petitions and Requests:** There are many examples given in the Bible. Here are but a few:

- For our basic needs to be met.[29]
- For physical healing.[30,31]
- For strength[32] and boldness.[33]
- For wisdom[34] and guidance.[35,36]
- For help[37] and safety.[38]
- For protection from our enemies.[39]

Give us today our daily bread.
(Matthew 6:11)[29]

Is any one of you sick? He should call the elders of the church to pray over him and anoint him with oil in the name of the Lord. And the prayer offered in faith will make the sick person well; the Lord will raise him up.
(James 5:14-15)[30]

Therefore confess your sins to each other and pray for each other so that you may be healed.
(James 5:16)[31]

I pray that out of his glorious riches he may strengthen you with power through his Spirit in your inner being,
(Ephesians 3:16)[32]

When I called, you answered me; you made me bold and stouthearted.
(Psalm 138:3)[33]

If any of you lacks wisdom, he should ask God, who gives generously to all without finding fault, and it will be given to him.
(James 1:5)[34]

Show me your ways, O LORD, teach me your paths.
(Psalm 25:4)[35]

You guide me with your counsel, and afterward you will take me into glory.
(Psalm 73:24)[36]

Come quickly to help me, O Lord my Savior.
(Psalm 38:22)[37]

- For one another.[40,41]
- For those who persecute[42] or mistreat us.[43]
- For evangelism.[44-47]

Keep me safe, O God, for in you I take refuge.
(Psalm 16:1)[38]

Hide me in the shadow of your wings from the wicked
who assail me, from my mortal enemies who surround me.
(Psalm 17:8-9)[39]

Therefore confess your sins to each other and pray for each other
so that you may be healed.
(James 5:16)[40]

I urge you, brothers, by our Lord Jesus Christ and by the love of
the Spirit, to join me in my struggle by praying to God for me.
(Romans 15:30)[41]

*But I tell you: Love your enemies and pray for those who persecute
you, that you may be sons of your Father in heaven.*
(Matthew 5:44)[42]

Bless those who curse you, pray for those who mistreat you.
(Luke 6:28)[43]

Pray also for me, that whenever I open my mouth, words may be
given me so that I will fearlessly make known the mystery of the
gospel.
(Ephesians 6:19)[44]

And pray for us, too, that God may open a door for our message,
so that we may proclaim the mystery of Christ,
for which I am in chains.
(Colossians 4:3)[45]

Finally, brothers, pray for us that the message of the Lord may
spread rapidly and be honored, just as it was with you.
(2 Thessalonians 3:1)[46]

Then he [Jesus] said to his disciples, *"The harvest is plentiful
but the workers are few. Ask the Lord of the harvest, therefore,
to send out workers into his harvest field."*
(Matthew 9:37-38)[47]

4. **Confession and Forgiveness:** We confess our sins and pray that our sins will be forgiven—just as we have forgiven those who have sinned against us.[48-50]

5. **Deliverance from Temptation and the Power of the Devil**: We pray that we will not fall into temptation and that we will be delivered from the evil one [the devil].[51-53]

There is no "magic formula" for prayer—no exclusive "posture" or preferred method for approaching and drawing near to God. The Bible reveals that Jesus sometimes knelt when He prayed.[54] At other times He prayed while standing and looking up,[55] or bowing down with His face to the ground.[56] At times He prayed in public.[57]

<u>Forgive us our debts, as we also have forgiven our debtors.</u>
(Matthew 6:12)[48]

If we confess our sins, he is faithful and just to forgive us our sins, and purify us from all unrighteousness.
(1 John 1:9)[49]

Then I acknowledged my sin to you and did not cover up my iniquity. I said, "I will confess my transgressions to the LORD"—and you forgave the guilt of my sin.
(Psalm 32:5)[50]

*<u>And lead us not into temptation,
but deliver us from the evil one.</u>*
(Matthew 6:13)[51]

Watch and pray that you will not fall into temptation. The spirit is willing, but the body is weak.
(Matthew 26:41)[52]

My prayer is not that you take them out of this world but that you protect them from the evil one.
(John 17:15)[53]

He [Jesus] withdrew about a stone's throw beyond them, knelt down and prayed.
(Luke 22:41)[54]

After Jesus said this, he looked toward heaven and prayed.
(John 17:1)[55]

At other times He pulled away from His disciples, and prayed by Himself, alone and far away from others.[58,59]

It appears that Jesus may have had an established pattern of getting up early in the morning to pray.[60] However, He also prayed at night and on at least one occasion, He went out to a mountain top and prayed all night to His heavenly Father.[61]

Although prayer can take place under many different circumstances and take many different forms, not all prayers are equally acceptable in God's sight. There are many different hindrances to prayer mentioned in the Bible. All of the factors cited below may seriously impede God's answers to our prayers:

- **Sin**: God does not easily listen to the prayers of sinners; those who are unrepentant and who willfully cherish sin in their hearts.[62-64]

Going a little farther, he [Jesus] fell to the ground and prayed that if possible the hour might pass from him. **(Mark 14:35)**[56]

At that time Jesus, full of joy through the Holy Spirit, said, *"I praise you, Father, Lord of heaven and earth, because you have hidden these things from the wise and learned, and revealed them to little children. Yes, Father, for this was your good pleasure.*
(Luke 10:21)[57]

But Jesus often withdrew to lonely places and prayed. **(Luke 5:16)**[58]

After leaving them, he [Jesus] went up on a mountainside to pray. **(Mark 6:46)**[59]

Very early in the morning, while it was still dark, Jesus got up, left the house and went off to a solitary place, where he prayed. **(Mark 1:35)**[60]

One of those days Jesus went out to a mountainside to pray, and spent the night praying to God. **(Luke 6:12)**[61]

If I had cherished sin in my heart, the Lord would not have listened. **(Psalm 66:18)**[62]

We know that God does not listen to sinners. **(John 9:31)**[63]

But your iniquities have separated you from your God; your sins have hidden his face from you, so that he will not hear.
(Isaiah 59:2)[64]

- **Ignoring God's Laws:** If you turn a "deaf ear" to God's laws, as contained in the Bible, your prayers are detestable to Him.[65]

- **Wickedness:** God distances Himself from the prayers of evil or wicked people.[66]

- **Wrong Motives:** God cannot be fooled. If you pray with the wrong motives (for example, asking for money for others, when you really want the money for yourself), you will not receive an answer to your prayer.[67]

- **Doubt and Lack of Faith:** If you doubt God's existence or question His power to answer prayers, do not expect to receive anything from the Lord when you pray.[68,69]

- **Selfishness**: If you are selfish and ignore those who are poor or needy, do not expect to receive blessings when you, yourself, cry out for help.[70]

If anyone turns a deaf ear to the law,
even his prayers are detestable.
(Proverbs 28:9)[65]

The LORD is far from the wicked but he hears the
prayer of the righteous.
(Proverbs 15:29)[66]

When you ask, you do not receive, because you ask
with wrong motives, that you may spend what you get on
your own pleasures.
(James 4:3)[67]

But when he asks, he must believe and not doubt, because
he who doubts is like a wave of the sea, blown and tossed
by the wind. That man should not think he will receive
anything from the Lord; he is a double-minded man,
unstable in all he does.
(James 1:6-7)[68]

And without faith it is impossible to please God, because
anyone who comes to him must believe that he exists and
that he rewards those who earnestly seek him.
(Hebrews 11:6)[69]

- **Arrogance/Pride**: God distances Himself from people who are arrogant; He hates and opposes those who are prideful.[71-73]

- **Unforgiveness:** When you stand before God praying, if you hold anything against anyone, you must forgive and "let go" of everything; otherwise, your Father in heaven will not forgive your sins when you confess them.[74,75]

- **Disharmony in the Home:** If you mistreat your spouse, your prayers may be hindered.[76]

If a man shuts his ears to the cry of the poor,
he too will cry out and not be answered.
(Proverbs 21:13)[70]

Israel's arrogance testifies against them; the Israelites,
even Ephraim, stumble in their sin; Judah also stumbles
with them. When they go with their flocks and herds
to seek the LORD, they will not find him;
he has withdrawn himself from them.
(Hosea 5:5-6)[71]

The LORD detests all the proud of heart.
(Proverbs 16:5)[72]

God opposes the proud but gives grace to the humble.
(James 4:6)[73]

*And when you stand praying, if you hold anything
against anyone, forgive him, so that your Father
in heaven may forgive you your sins.*
(Mark 11:25)[74]

*For if you forgive men when they sin against you, your heavenly
Father will also forgive you. But if you do not forgive men
their sins, your Father will not forgive your sins.*
(Matthew 6:14-15)[75]

Husbands, in the same way be considerate as you live
with your wives, and treat them with respect as the weaker
partner and as heirs with you of the gracious gift of life,
so that nothing will hinder your prayers.
(1 Peter 3:7)[76]

- **Hypocrisy:** Jesus spoke out against the religious legalists of His time who prayed lengthy and showy prayers in public, while behind the scenes they took advantage of the defenseless.[77-79]

God's Guidance

Although there are a number of hindrances to prayer, the Bible also contains reference to several factors that promote a successful prayer life:

- **Having Strong Faith and Belief:** God hears our prayers and answers them when our faith and belief are strong.[80-82]

- **Being Obedient:** If we have a clear conscience and obey God's commands, God says He will give us anything we ask for in prayer.[83]

And when you pray, do not be like the hypocrites, for they love to pray standing in the synagogues and on the street corners to be seen by men.
(Matthew 6:5)[77]

And when you pray, do not keep babbling like pagans, for they think they will be heard because of their many words.
(Matthew 6:7)[78]

They devour widows' houses and for a show make lengthy prayers. Such men will be punished most severely.
(Mark 12:40)[79]

If you believe, you will receive whatever you ask for in prayer.
(Matthew 21:22)[80]

If you have faith as small as a mustard seed, you can say to this mulberry tree, "Be uprooted and planted in the sea," and it will obey you.
(Luke 17:6)[81]

I tell you the truth, if anyone says to this mountain, "Go throw yourself into the sea," and does not doubt in his heart but believes that what he says will happen, it will be done for him. Therefore I tell you, whatever you ask for in prayer, believe that you have received it, and it will be yours.
(Mark 11:22-24)[82]

- **Being Righteous:** God is especially attentive to the prayers of people who are righteous; their prayers are powerful and effective, and God promises to deliver them from all their troubles.[84-86]

- **Being Humble:** God hears us and responds favorably when we come before Him in humility.[87-89]

- **Seeking God's Will:** Our Lord listens to godly people who do His will;[90] if we ask for anything that is consistent with

---

Dear friends, if our hearts do not condemn us, we have confidence before God and receive from him anything we ask, because we obey his commands and do what pleases him.
(1 John 3:21-22)[83]

The prayer of a righteous man is powerful and effective.
(James 5:16)[84]

The righteous cry out, and the LORD hears them; he delivers them from all their troubles.
(Psalm 34:17)[85]

For the eyes of the Lord are on the righteous and his ears are attentive to their prayer, but the face of the Lord is against those who do evil.
(1 Peter 3:12)[86]

Humble yourselves before the Lord, and he will lift you up.
(James 4:10)[87]

If my people, who are called by my name, will humble themselves and pray and seek my face and turn from their wicked ways, then will I hear from heaven and forgive their sin and will heal their land.
(2 Chronicles 7:14)[88]

Because your heart was responsive and you humbled yourself before God when you heard what he spoke against this place and its people, and because you humbled yourself before me and tore your robes and wept in my presence, I have heard you, declares the LORD.
(2 Chronicles 34:27)[89]

He [God] listens to the godly man who does his will.
(John 9:31)[90]

His will, He hears us.[91] Therefore, it is important that we pray to understand God's will for our lives.[92,93]

- **Abiding in Christ:** When the words of Christ abide in our heart, we will naturally pray for that which Christ will honor. When we pray in accordance with this indwelling of Christ, we can ask for anything and it will be given to us.[94]

- **Praying in the Name of Jesus:** Christ promised that if we pray "in his name" we will receive whatever we ask for and "our joy will be complete." Praying in the name of Jesus implies oneness with Christ in heart and will. Both Jesus and God respond to prayers that are consistent with the character of Christ.[95,96]

- **Praying in Secret:** To avoid hypocrisy, Christ recommended we go into a room, close the door, and pray to God in secret. When God sees what you have done in secret, He will reward you.[97]

This is the confidence we have in approaching God:
that if we ask anything according to his will, he hears us.
(1 John 5:14)[91]

Therefore do not be foolish, but understand
what the Lord's will is.
(Ephesians 5:17)[92]

We have not stopped praying for you and asking God to
fill you with the knowledge of his will through all spiritual
wisdom and understanding.
(Colossians 1:9)[93]

*If you remain in me and my words remain in you,
ask whatever you wish, and it will be given to you.*
(John 15:7)[94]

*And I will do whatever you ask in my name, so that the
Son may bring glory to the Father. You may ask me
for anything in my name, and I will do it.*
(John 14:13-14)[95]

*I tell you the truth, my Father will give you whatever you ask
in my name...Ask and you will receive,
and your joy will be complete.*
(John 16:23,24)[96]

- **Praying Through the Holy Spirit:** Praying through the Spirit is one of the most powerful and effective means we have of approaching God. When we don't know what to pray, or how to pray, we can draw upon the Holy Spirit to assist us in our prayers.

    The Holy Spirit prays within us, and for us, in accordance with God's will. Intercession by the Spirit can transcend beyond the level of words.[98] God will fully understand these prayers, even if words are not used. In order to receive the gift of the Holy Spirit, all we need to do is to ask God.[99]

Of all the things mentioned thus far, arguably the most important factor that will determine the "success" of our prayers, is whether or not the things we ask for are consistent with God's intentional will for our lives (or for the life of the person or persons for whom we are praying).

That is, no matter how much we want something to happen, and no matter how earnest our requests to God may be, we must always defer to God's will for our lives, and accept His answer—even if the answer is "No." This point was clearly and profoundly

---

But when you pray, go into your room, close the door and pray to your Father, who is unseen. Then your Father, who sees what is done in secret, will reward you.
(Matthew 6:6)[97]

In the same way, the Spirit helps us in our weakness. We do not know what we ought to pray for, but the Spirit himself intercedes for us with groans that words cannot express. And he who searches our hearts knows the mind of the Spirit, because the Spirit intercedes for the saints in accordance with God's will.
(Romans 8:26-28)[98]

If you then, though you are evil, know how to give good gifts to your children, how much more will your Father in heaven give the Holy Spirit to those who ask him!
(Luke 11:13)[99]

demonstrated by Jesus Christ when, in the Garden of Gethsemane, He prayed to God the Father to save Him from death by crucifixion.[100-102]

In the end, Christ's prayer was not answered (presumably because it was not in accordance with God's will). All of mankind benefited when Christ (despite His repeated and fervent prayer to God) ultimately submitted to His Father's will, and was crucified for our salvation.[103] This act of submission to God's will is a perfect example of how we should live our own lives.

Finally, it is important to remember that Christ's death was only temporary. He was raised from the dead after the third day and He lives forever at the right hand of God.[104] Obviously, something incredibly good can ultimately result when we submit our will to God's will.

Going a little farther, he fell with his face to the ground and prayed, *"My Father, if it is possible, may this cup be taken from me. Yet not as I will, but as you will."*
(Matthew 26:39)[100]

He went away a second time and prayed,
"My Father, if it is not possible for this cup to be taken away unless I drink it, may your will be done."
(Matthew 26:42)[101]

So he [Jesus] left them and went away once more and prayed the third time, saying the same thing.
(Matthew 26:44)[102]

He himself bore our sins in his body on the tree, so that we might die to sins and live for righteousness; by his wounds you have been healed.
(1 Peter 2:24)[103]

But from now on, the Son of Man will be seated at the right hand of the mighty God.
(Luke 22:69)[104]

Lesson 23

Pride

"This is the one I esteem: He who is humble and contrite in spirit, and trembles at my word."
(Isaiah 66:2)

Pride: self-aggrandizing, arrogant, or disdainful conduct or treatment; haughtiness

Pride is one of God's least favorite characteristics of human beings. He loves the humble, but talks strongly against the prideful. Pride typically leads to disaster, but humility leads to blessings. If you are prideful, you need to change your attitude and humble yourself before the Lord and before others, just as Jesus Christ humbled Himself for all humanity.

Synopsis

God "detests" the prideful[1] and promises that there will be a day when all people who are proud will be humbled.[2,3] If you have a prideful heart, you cannot hide it from God; the Lord judges our

---

The LORD detests all the proud of heart.
(Proverbs 16:5)[1]

The LORD Almighty has a day in store
for all the proud and lofty,
for all that is exalted (and they will be humbled).
(Isaiah 2:12)[2]

The arrogance of man will be brought low
and the pride of men humbled.
(Isaiah 2:17)[3]

inmost thoughts.[4] And His judgment can be harsh. Pride often leads to the destruction[5] and the downfall of the individual.[6] God does not tolerate pride,[7] and a prideful heart distances us from God.[8]

People who are prideful love to get praise and attention from others; in fact, they love the praise of men more than they love praise from God.[9] In addition, prideful people love themselves so much that their pride interferes with their ability to detect their own sin.[10] Their haughty behavior often leads to arguments and quarrels with others, and they typically fail to take advice when it is given[11] (Why do you need advice if you are almost perfect?).

> He has scattered those who are proud in their inmost thoughts. He has brought down rulers from their thrones, but has lifted up the humble.
> **(Luke 1:51-52)**[4]

> Pride goes before destruction, a haughty spirit before a fall.
> **(Proverbs 16:18)**[5]

> Before his downfall, a man's heart is proud, but humility comes before honor.
> **(Proverbs 18:12)**[6]

> Whoever has haughty eyes and a proud heart, him will I not endure.
> **(Psalm 101:5)**[7]

> Though the Lord is on high, he looks upon the lowly, but the proud he knows from afar.
> **(Psalm 138:6)**[8]

> For they loved praise from men more than praise from God.
> **(John 12:43)**[9]

> For in his own eyes he flatters himself too much to detect or hate his sin.
> **(Psalm 36:2)**[10]

> Pride only breeds quarrels, but wisdom is found in those who take advice.
> **(Proverbs 13:10)**[11]

God's Guidance

The antidote for pride is humility. God holds in high regard, people who are humble.[12] This is not surprising, since humility is a cardinal feature of the personality of Jesus Christ.[13] Jesus humbled Himself for all human beings when, although He was equal to God, He came to earth and lived as a servant and died for our sins.[14] The Bible encourages us to adopt the same attitude of humility as shown by the actions of Jesus Christ.[14]

As Christians, we are commanded to "clothe ourselves in humility" toward one another,[15] and never think of ourselves as being better than anyone else,[16] or look down on someone because of their "low position" or station in life.[17] In fact, we are to honor others more

---

This is the one I esteem: He who is humble and
contrite in spirit, and trembles at my word.
(Isaiah 66:2)[12]

*Take my yoke upon you and learn from me,
for I am gentle and humble in heart,
and you will find rest for your souls.*
(Matthew 11:29)[13]

Your attitude should be the same as that of Christ Jesus:
Who, being in very nature God, did not consider equality with
God something to be grasped, but made himself nothing,
taking the very nature of a servant,
being made in human likeness.
(Philippians 2:5-7)[14]

All of you, clothe yourselves with humility toward one
another, because, "God opposes the proud,
but gives grace to the humble."
(1 Peter 5:5)[15]

Do nothing out of selfish ambition or vain conceit,
but in humility consider others better than yourselves.
(Philippians 2:3)[16]

Do not be proud, but be willing to associate with people
of low position. Do not be conceited.
(Romans 12:16)[17]

than we honor ourselves,[18] and consider others to be better than ourselves.[19]

In God's eyes, we are foolish if we think of ourselves more highly than we should.[20,21] Also, He advises against a life that focuses on receiving honor and praise from others.[22]

God holds in high esteem those who are humble and have a contrite spirit.[23] In the end, it is humility and fear of the Lord that bring wealth and honor and life.[24] It is the meek who will inherit the land and enjoy great peace.[25]

Honor one another above yourselves.
(Romans 12:10)[18]

Do nothing out of selfish ambition or vain conceit,
but in humility consider others better than yourselves.
(Philippians 2:3)[19]

Do not think of yourselves more highly than you ought,
but rather think of yourself with sober judgment,
in accordance with the measure of faith
God has given you.
(Romans 12:3)[20]

If you have played the fool and exalted yourself,
or if you have planned evil,
clap your hand over your mouth!
(Proverbs 30:32)[21]

It is not good to eat too much honey,
nor is it honorable to seek one's own honor.
(Proverbs 25:27)[22]

This is the one I esteem: he who is humble and contrite
in spirit, and trembles at my word.
(Isaiah 66:2)[23]

Humility and fear of the Lord bring
wealth and honor and life.
(Proverbs 22:4)[24]

But the meek will inherit the land
and enjoy great peace.
(Psalm 37:11)[25]

Lesson 23

Self-Esteem, Low

"The Spirit of God has made me; the breath
of the Almighty gives me life."
(Job 33:4)

Self-Esteem: the appraised value or worth of oneself

Despite biblical evidence to the contrary, many Christians have extremely low self-esteem. They have listened to the lies that the world has taught them, and believe they are dumb, ugly, unimportant, worthless, etc. The Bible paints an entirely different view of Christians.

As Christians, it is important to realize that we are extremely valuable in God's eyes. Understanding who you are in Christ can be critically important to a mentally healthy life. The following is a partial list of Scriptures that relate to your value and worth in the sight of God.

WHO I AM

I AM A CHILD OF GOD

You are all sons of God through faith in Christ Jesus.
(Galatians 3:26)

Yet to all who received him [Jesus Christ], to those who believed in his name, he gave the right to become children of God.
(John 1:12)

And by him we cry, "Abba, Father." The Spirit testifies with our spirit that we are God's children.
(Romans 8:15-16)

I AM MADE IN GOD'S IMAGE

So God created man in his own image,
in the image of God he created him;
male and female he created them.
(Genesis 1:27)

I AM GOD'S TEMPLE

Don't you know that you yourselves are God's temple and that God's Spirit lives in you?
(1 Corinthians 3:16)

I AM A WONDERFUL HAND-MADE

For you created my inmost being; you knit me
together in my mother's womb.
(Psalm 139:13)

I praise you because I am fearfully and
wonderfully made.
(Psalm 139:14)

I AM ONLY "A LITTLE LOWER THAN THE HEAVENLY BEINGS"

You made him [man] a little lower than
the heavenly beings and crowned
him with glory and honor.
(Psalm 8:5)

I AM CHRIST'S AMBASSADOR ON

We are therefore Christ's ambassadors, as though
God were making his appeal through us.
(2 Corinthians 5:20)

As God's fellow workers, we urge you not
to receive God's grace in vain.
(2 Corinthians 6:1)

I AM A CITIZEN OF

But our citizenship is in heaven. And we
eagerly await a Savior from there,
the Lord Jesus Christ.
(Philippians 3:20)

I AM A NEW CREATION IN

Therefore, if anyone is in Christ, he is a new
creation; the old has gone, the new has come!
(2 Corinthians 5:17)

I AM BEING TRANSFORMED INTO CHRIST'S LIKENESS

And we, who with unveiled faces all reflect the Lord's glory,
are being transformed into his likeness with ever-increasing
glory, which comes from the Lord, who is the Spirit.
(2 Corinthians 3:18)

And just as we have borne the likeness of the earthly man,
so shall we bear the likeness of the man from heaven.
(1 Corinthians 15:49)

In this way, love is made complete among us so that
we will have confidence on the day of judgment,
because in this world we are like him.
(1 John 4:17)

I AM GOD'S WORKMANSHIP

For we are God's workmanship, created in Christ Jesus
to do good works, which God prepared
in advance for us to do.
(Ephesians 2:10)

I AM CHRIST'S FRIEND

*I no longer call you servants...Instead, I have called
you friends, for everything that I learned from
my Father I have made known to you.*
(John 15:15)

I HAVE BEEN CHOSEN BY GOD

*You did not choose me, but I chose you and appointed you to go
and bear fruit—fruit that will last. Then the father will give
you whatever you ask in my name.*
(John 15:16)

He appointed us, set his seal of ownership on us,
and put his Spirit in our hearts as a deposit,
guaranteeing what is to come.
(2 Corinthians 1:21-22)

I AM A SAINT

Paul, an apostle of Christ Jesus by the will of God,
To the saints in Ephesus, the
faithful in Christ Jesus.
(Ephesians 1:1)

I AM A MEMBER OF CHRIST'S

Now you are the body of Christ, and
each one of you is a part of it.
(1 Corinthians 12:27)

*I am the vine; you are the branches. If a man remains
in me and I in him, he will bear much fruit.*
(John 15:5)

GOD LISTENS TO MY PRAYERS

This is the confidence we have in approaching God:
that if we ask anything according to
his will, he hears us.
(1 John 5:14)

*I tell you the truth, my Father will give you
whatever you ask in my name.*
(John 16:23)

I AM AN HEIR TO THE KINGDOM OF GOD

Now if we are children, then we are heirs—heirs of God
and co-heirs with Christ, if indeed we share
in his sufferings in order that we
may also share in his glory.
(Romans 8:17)

Having believed, you were marked in him with a seal,
the promised Holy Spirit, who is a deposit guaranteeing
our inheritance until the redemption of those who are
God's possession—to the praise of his glory.
(Ephesians 1:13-14)

I AM STRONG IN CHRIST

I can do everything through him [Christ]
who gives me strength.
(Philippians 4:13)

CHRIST DIED FOR ME

But God demonstrates his own love for us
in this: While we were still sinners,
Christ died for us.
(Romans 5:8)

I AM FORGIVEN

Blessed is the man whose sin the Lord will
never count against him.
(Romans 4:8)

*So if the Son sets you free [from sin],
you will be free indeed.*
(John 8:36)

I AM FREE OF CONDEMNATION

Therefore, there is now no condemnation
for those who are in Christ Jesus.
(Romans 8:1)

THE HOLY SPIRIT LIVES IN ME

God has poured out his love into our hearts
by the Holy Spirit, whom he has given us.
(Romans 5:5)

The Spirit gives life; the flesh counts for nothing.
(John 6:63)

I AM RIGHTEOUS, BLAMELESS, AND HOLY BEFORE GOD

Christ is the end of the law so that there may be
righteousness for everyone who believes.
(Romans 10:4)

But if Christ is in you, your body is dead because of sin,
yet your spirit is alive because of righteousness.
(Romans 8:10)

But now that you have been set free from sin and
have become slaves to God, the benefit you reap
leads to holiness, and the result is eternal life.
(Romans 6:22)

For he chose us in him before the creation
of the world to be holy and blameless
in his sight.
(Ephesians 1:4)

I AM LOVED BY GOD

*For God so loved the world that he gave his one and only Son,
that whoever believes in him shall not perish
but have eternal life.*
(John 3:16)

This is love: not that we loved God, but the he loved us
and sent his Son as an atoning sacrifice for our sins.
(1 John 4:10)

I CANNOT BE SEPARATED FROM GOD'S LOVE

For I am convinced that neither death nor life,
neither angels nor demons, neither the present
nor the future, nor any powers, neither height
nor depth, nor anything else in all creation,
will be able to separate us from the love of
God that is in Christ Jesus our Lord.
(Romans 8:38-39)

Lesson 25

Sexual Sin

*"The body is not meant for sexual immorality,
but for the Lord and the Lord for the body."*
(1 Corinthians 6:13)

Sex: anything pertaining to sexual gratification or reproduction

God's design is for sexual intercourse to occur exclusively between one man and one woman within the context of marriage. Sexual activity outside of marriage is considered sinful and condemned by God.

Synopsis

God's Plan for Sexuality:

After God created man and woman, He blessed them and told them to be fruitful and multiply and fill the earth.[1] It is God's plan that men and women marry, be united together sexually and become one flesh,[2] so that they are no longer two, but one.[3]

God blessed them and said to them, "Be fruitful and increase
in number; fill the earth and subdue it."
(Genesis 1:28)[1]

For this reason a man will leave his father and mother and be
united to his wife, and they will become one flesh.
(Genesis 2:24)[2]

So they are no longer two, but one.
(Mark 10:8)[3]

The wife's body does not belong to her alone but also to
her husband. In the same way, the husband's body does
not belong to him alone but also to his wife.
(1 Corinthians 7:4)[4]

As a result of the marital union, the husband's body is no longer his alone (but also the wife's), and the wife's body is no longer hers alone (but also her husband's).[4]

Each spouse is instructed to fulfill the other's sexual needs, and not deprive one other—so that neither husband nor wife will fall into sexual temptation.[5] The marriage bed is intended to be kept pure: sexual activity outside of marriage is strictly prohibited.[6]

Scriptures on Sexual Sin:

Adultery: Although it is God's desire that sex occur exclusively within marriage, human beings have difficulty adhering to this standard. Perhaps the most prominent sexual sin mentioned in the Bible is that of adultery.[6] In the Seventh Commandment, God proclaims: "You shall not commit adultery."[7] If any one does so, his/her act will not go unpunished by God.[8]

In addition to adultery, the Scriptures specifically condemn having sex with prostitutes.[9] Prostitutes can be seductive and lure people

> Do not deprive each other except by mutual consent and for a time, so that you may devote yourselves to prayer. Then come together again so that Satan will not tempt you because of your lack of self-control.
> **(1 Corinthians 7:5)**[5]
>
> A man who commits adultery lacks judgment; whoever does so destroys himself.
> **(Proverbs 6:32)**[6]
>
> "You shall not commit adultery."
> **(Exodus 20:14)**[7]
>
> Can a man scoop fire into his lap without his clothes being burned? Can a man walk on hot coals without his feet being scorched? So is he who sleeps with another man's wife; no one who touches her will go unpunished.
> **(Proverbs 6:27-29)**[8]
>
> Do you not know that your bodies are members of Christ himself? Shall I then take the members of Christ and unite them with a prostitute? Never!
> **(1 Corinthians 6:15)**[9]

into temptation and sin.[10] If you have sex with a prostitute, you become "one flesh" with the prostitute, just as husband and wife become one flesh through the act of sexual union.[11]

Homosexuality: Homosexuality (whether male[12] or female[13]) is also condemned by God. Such actions are referred to as "detestable"[14] and the people who engage in them as "wicked."[15] The apostle Paul states that men who commit such indecent acts "received in themselves the due penalty for their perversion."[16] Most importantly, homosexual behavior, if willful and unrepentant, may seriously call into question one's eternal salvation."[15]

Other Perversions: In addition to homosexuality, other forms of sexual perversion[16] and sexual sin are also condemned in the Bible,

---

Do not let your heart turn to her ways or stray into her paths.
Many are the victims she has brought down; her slain
are a mighty throng.
(Proverbs 7:25-26)[10]

Do you not know that he who unites himself with a prostitute
is one with her in body? For it is said, "The two will become
one flesh." But he who unites himself with the Lord
is one with him in spirit.
(1 Corinthians 6:16-17)[11]

In the same way the men also abandoned natural relations with
women and were inflamed with lust for one another.
(Romans 1:27)[12]

Because of this, God gave them over to shameful lusts. Even
their women exchanged natural relations for unnatural ones.
(Romans 1:26)[13]

Do not lie with a man as one lies with a woman; that is detestable.
(Leviticus 18:22)[14]

Do you not know that the wicked will not inherit the kingdom
of God? Do not be deceived: Neither the sexually immoral
nor idolaters nor adulterers nor male prostitutes nor homosexual offenders nor thieves nor the greedy nor drunkards nor
slanderers nor swindlers will inherit the kingdom of God.
(1 Corinthians 6:9-10)[15]

Men committed indecent acts with other men, and received in
themselves the due penalty for their perversion.
(Romans 1:27)[16]

including: cross-dressing[17] (a man wearing women's clothing, or a woman wearing men's clothing); beastiality[18,19] (having sexual relations with an animal); and sex with close relatives (incest).[20]

Pornography: Although the term "pornography" is not mentioned in Scriptures, the Bible clearly indicates that we are to control our eyes,[21] and not look lustfully upon others.[22,23] Jesus commented that if you look lustfully upon a woman, you have already committed adultery with her.[24]

Pedophilia: Finally, although the sexual disorder called "pedophilia" (having sex with young children) is not specifically mentioned in the Bible, Jesus Christ spoke indirectly to this topic. Jesus loved young children, and was especially protective of them.

A woman must not wear men's clothing, nor a man wear women's clothing, for the LORD your God detests anyone who does this.
(Deuteronomy 22:5)[17]

"Cursed is the man who has sexual relations with any animal."
(Deuteronomy 27:21)[18]

A woman must not present herself to an animal to have sexual relations with it; that is a perversion.
(Leviticus 18:23)[19]

"No one is to approach any close relative to have sexual relations. I am the LORD."
(Leviticus 18:6)[20]

I made a covenant with my eyes not to look lustfully at a girl.
(Job 31:1)[21]

Put to death, therefore, whatever belongs to your earthly nature: sexual immorality, impurity, lust, evil desires and greed, which is idolatry.
(Colossians 3:5)[22]

Do not lust in your heart after her beauty or let her captivate you with her eyes, for the prostitute reduces you to a loaf of bread, and the adulteress preys upon your very life.
(Proverbs 6:25-26)[23]

But I tell you that anyone who looks at a woman lustfully has already committed adultery with her in his heart.
(Matthew 5:28)[24]

Jesus proclaimed:

"But if anyone causes one of these little ones who believe in me to sin, it would be better for him to have a large millstone hung around his neck and to be drowned in the depths of the sea."[25]

God's Guidance

The Bible tells us that the body was not meant for sexual immorality, but for the Lord.[26] Our bodies were bought for a price,[27] and that price was the sacrificial death of Jesus Christ, who died for our salvation. Our bodies are a temple of the Holy Spirit, and we are to honor God with our bodies[27] and live holy lives.[28]

We are to learn to control our lusts and sexual desires.[29] We are to flee from all sexual immorality[30] and put to death that which be-

---

But if anyone causes one of these little ones who believe in me to sin, it would be better for him to have a large millstone hung around his neck and to be drowned in the depths of the sea.
(Matthew 18:6)[25]

The body is not meant for sexual immorality,
but for the Lord and the Lord for the body.
(1 Corinthians 6:13)[26]

Do you not know that your body is a temple of the Holy Spirit, who is in you, whom you have received from God? You are not your own; you were bought at a price. Therefore honor God with your body.
(1 Corinthians 6:19-20)[27]

For God did not call us to be impure, but to live a holy life.
(1 Thessalonians 4:7)[28]

It is God's will that you should be sanctified: that you should avoid sexual immorality; that each of you should learn to control his own body in a way that is holy and honorable, not in passionate lust like the heathen.
(1 Thessalonians 4:3-5)[29]

Flee from sexual immorality. All other sins a man commits are outside his body, but he who sins sexually sins against his own body.
(1 Corinthians 6:18)[30]

longs to our sinful nature.[31] We are to learn to control our bodies in a way that is holy and honorable.[29] We are to be self-controlled and live such pure lives that there is not even a hint of sexual immorality or impurity.[32] Those who belong to Jesus Christ have crucified the sinful nature with its passions and desires.[33]

We are to teach young people to be self-controlled,[34] and we ourselves are to flee the evil desires of our youth.[35] As we mature in Christ, we are to pursue righteousness.[35] The Bible reminds us that we cannot hide our sexual sin from God; a man's ways are in full view of the Lord.[36] Even our sinful thoughts are known to God.[37]

> For if you live according to the sinful nature,
> you will die; but if by the Spirit you put to death
> the misdeeds of the body, you will live.
> **(Romans 8:13)**[31]
>
> But among you there must not be even a hint of sexual immorality, or of any kind of impurity, or of greed, because these are improper for God's holy people.
> **(Ephesians 5:3)**[32]
>
> Those who belong to Christ Jesus have crucified the sinful nature with its passions and desires.
> **(Galatians 5:24)**[33]
>
> Encourage the young men to be self-controlled.
> **(Titus 2:6)**[34]
>
> Flee the evil desires of youth, and pursue righteousness, faith, love and peace, along with those who call on the Lord out of a pure heart.
> **(2 Timothy 2:22)**[35]
>
> For a man's ways are in full view of the Lord,
> and he examines all his paths.
> **(Proverbs 5:21)**[36]
>
> The Lord detests the thoughts of the wicked,
> but those of the pure are pleasing to him.
> **(Proverbs 15:26)**[37]

If you are caught in sexual sin, you are to repent and turn back to the Lord.[38] You are to come to your senses, and stop sinning.[39] If you sincerely repent, and ask for forgiveness, God will forgive your sins and cleanse you from all iniquity.[40] However, if you deliberately and willfully keep on sinning, after you have received knowledge of the truth, Christ's sacrifice for your sins no longer applies, and you are in danger of God's judgment and eternity in hell.[41]

> Repent, then, and turn to God,
> so that your sins may be wiped out.
> **(Acts 3:19-20)**[38]
>
> Come back to your senses as you ought,
> and stop sinning.
> **(1 Corinthians 15:34)**[39]
>
> Wash away all my iniquity and cleanse me from my sin.
> **(Psalm 51:2)**[40]
>
> If we deliberately keep on sinning after we have received
> the knowledge of the truth, no sacrifice for sins is left,
> but only a fearful expectation of judgment and of raging fire
> that will consume the enemies of God.
> **(Hebrews 10:26-27)**[41]

Lesson 26

SIN

"There will be trouble and distress for every human being who does evil."
(Romans 2:9)

Sin: breaking God's moral laws (sins of *commission*) or failing to act according to God's teachings (sins of *omission*)

Sin dominates the picture of our modern world—murder, rape, infidelity, drug abuse, lying, deception, and stealing, are commonplace. Everywhere we turn we see evidence of man's inhumanity to man and the glaring failure of human beings to take action and do what is right.

Every human being sins, and we all experience the harmful consequences of our sin as we live in this world. Without the sacrifice of Christ on the cross, our sins would separate us from God and we would live for eternity in Hell. But hallelujah! Christ came into this world to die for our sins, so that our sins would not be counted against us. Those who repent and believe in Christ, and God who sent Him, inherit eternal life and will dwell in the house of the Lord forever.

Synopsis

According to the Bible, we sin when we break God's moral law,[1] or when we fail to do the things we ought to do based on God's teachings.[2]

Everyone who sins breaks the law; in fact, sin is lawlessness.
(1 John 3:4)[1]

Anyone, then, who knows the good he ought to do and doesn't do it, sins.
(James 4:17)[2]

Lucifer, renamed Satan (also "devil"), was the original source of sin. One of the most powerful angels in heaven, Lucifer desired to be equal to God, and that was his downfall. He was banished from Heaven by God only to appear again in the Garden of Eden, where he tempted Adam and Eve to rebel against God (which they did when they ate of the forbidden fruit). Sin entered into this world through Adam's disobedience, and every human being since Adam has inherited the inclination to sin.[3]

We are all sinful from birth, from the time we are conceived.[4,5] No one is good except God alone.[6] If we claim to be without sin, then we are deceiving ourselves, and the truth is not in us.[7,8] There is no human being on earth who always does what is right and doesn't

---

Your first father sinned;
your spokesmen rebelled against me.
(Isaiah 43:27)[3]

Surely I was sinful at birth,
sinful from the time my mother conceived me.
(Psalm 51:5)[4]

I know that nothing good lives in me,
that is, in my sinful nature.
(Romans 7:18)[5]

No one is good—except God alone.
(Mark 10:18)[6]

If we claim to be without sin, we deceive ourselves
and the truth is not in us.
(1 John 1:8)[7]

If we claim we have not sinned,
we make him out to be a liar
and his word has no place in our lives.
(1 John 1:10)[8]

"Personal sin reflected upon
breeds compassion."
John M. Shanahan

sin.[9-11] In fact, if we claim we have not sinned, we will be judged by God for making that claim.[12]

Furthermore, as far as sin is concerned, no person is better than any other person. It doesn't matter how "good" you have been and how much of your life you have followed God's law; if you break just one law, you are guilty of breaking all of it.[13]

Unfortunately, there are always consequences for sin. If it were not for Christ's sacrifice on the cross (see below), the consequence for sin would be death—the spiritual separation of man from God. Although Christians are spared the ultimate judgment and condemnation for their sins, they still experience consequences for their sin while living on this earth.

In fact, all sins, no matter how "small" have consequences in this world. Some of our sins are obvious, and have immediate impacts, whereas the results of other sins are not apparent until some future point in time.[14]

But don't be fooled. We never "get away" with our sin. There will be trouble and distress for every human being who does evil.[15]

There is not a righteous man on earth
who does what is right and never sins.
(Ecclesiastes 7:20)[9]

Who can say, "I have kept my heart pure;
am clean and without sin"?
(Proverbs 20:9)[10]

All have turned aside, they have together become corrupt;
there is no one who does good, not even one.
(Psalm 14:3)[11]

But I will pass judgment on you because you say,
"I have not sinned."
(Jeremiah 2:35)[12]

For whoever keeps the whole law yet stumbles at just one point
is guilty of breaking all of it.
(James 2:10)[13]

The sins of some men are obvious, reaching the place of
judgment ahead of them; the sins of others trail behind them.
(1 Timothy 5:24)[14]

There is no peace for the wicked.[16] People who sin get trapped by their evil desires and find it hard to stop sinning.[17,18] Evil deeds are self-destructive and in the end we always end up being hurt by our own sinful actions.[19]

Sometimes it appears that God is "not fair" when it comes to sin; when we look around the world it seems that righteous men get what the wicked deserve and wicked men get what the righteous deserve.[20] But don't be deceived: God cannot be mocked. A man reaps what he sows.[21] Anyone who sows to please his sinful nature will reap destruction; the one who sows to please the Spirit reaps eternal life.[22]

There will be trouble and distress
for every human being who does evil.
(Romans 2:9)[15]

"There is no peace," says my God, "for the wicked."
(Isaiah 57:21)[16]

The righteousness of the upright delivers them,
but the unfaithful are trapped by evil desires.
(Proverbs 11:6)[17]

The evil deeds of a wicked man ensnare him;
the cords of his sin hold him fast.
(Proverbs 5:22)[18]

He who digs a hole and scoops it out falls into the pit he
has made. The trouble he causes recoils on himself;
his violence comes down on his own head.
(Psalm 7:15-16)[19]

There is something else meaningless that occurs on earth:
righteous men who get what the wicked deserve,
and wicked men who get what the righteous deserve.
(Ecclesiastes 8:14)[20]

Do not be deceived: God cannot be mocked.
A man reaps what he sows.
(Galatians 6:7)[21]

The one who sows to please his sinful nature, from that
nature will reap destruction; the one who sows to please
the Spirit, from the Spirit will reap eternal life.
(Galatians 6:8)[22]

In the final analysis, God is a just God and a jealous God. He laughs at the wicked, for He knows that their day of judgment is coming.[23] People who do evil have no hope for the future and will be "snuffed out" by God.[24] God watches over the righteous, but the way of the wicked will perish.[25] Things will always turn out better for God-fearing men who do what is right and are reverent before God.[26-28]

God's Guidance

Without Christ, our sin would hopelessly separate us from God. Christ was sent by God to pay the penalty for our sins.[29] He came

---

The Lord laughs at the wicked,
for he knows their day is coming.
(Psalm 37:13)[23]

The evil man has no future hope,
and the lamp of the wicked will be snuffed out.
(Proverbs 24:20)[24]

For the LORD watches over the way of the righteous,
but the way of the wicked will perish.
(Psalm 1:6)[25]

Although the wicked man commits a hundred crimes
and still lives a long time, I know that it will go better with
God-fearing men, who are reverent before God.
(Ecclesiastes 8:12)[26]

This is what the LORD says: "Maintain justice
and do what is right, for my salvation is close at hand
and my righteousness will soon be revealed.
(Isaiah 56:1)[27]

For I, the LORD your God, am a jealous God, punishing the
children for the sin of the fathers to the third and fourth
generation of those who hate me, but showing love
to a thousand generations of those who love me
and keep my commandments.
(Exodus 20:5-6)[28]

But you know that he [Christ] appeared so that he might
take away our sins.
(1 John 3:5)[29]

to earth to die for our sins so that our transgressions would not be counted against us.[30-33]

The only thing necessary to have our sins removed is to believe in Jesus Christ and confess (and repent of) our sins.[34,35] Those who believe in Jesus and repent are blessed, because their sins will be forgiven[36,37] and no longer be held against them.[38] Jesus wiped our

---

> God was reconciling the world to himself in Christ,
> not counting men's sins against them.
> **(2 Corinthians 5:19)**[30]
>
> This is love: not that we loved God, but that he loved us
> and sent his Son as an atoning sacrifice for our sins.
> **(1 John 4:10)**[31]
>
> He himself bore our sins in his body on the tree,
> so that we might die to sins and live for righteousness;
> by his wounds we have been healed.
> **(1 Peter 2:24)**[32]
>
> He was delivered over to death for our sins
> and was raised to life for our justification.
> **(Romans 4:25)**[33]
>
> If we confess our sins, he is faithful and just and will forgive us
> our sins and purify us from all unrighteousness.
> **(1 John 1:9)**[34]
>
> Repent, then, and turn to God, so that your sins may be wiped
> out, that times of refreshing may come from the Lord,
> and that he may send the Christ, who has been
> appointed for you—even Jesus.
> **(Acts 3:19-20)**[35]
>
> Everyone who believes in him receives forgiveness of sins
> through his name.
> **(Acts 10:43)**[36]
>
> *For God did not send his Son into the world to condemn the world,*
> *but to save the world through him. Whoever believes in him*
> *is not condemned.*
> **(John 3:17-18)**[37]
>
> Blessed is the man whose sin the Lord will
> never count against him.
> **(Romans 4:8)**[38]

accounts clean, and God is no longer aware of our sin.[39] Christ's sacrifice on the cross removes our sins as far as the east is from the west.[40]

Not only are our sins removed, when we believe in Jesus and confess our sins, the Holy Spirit comes to dwell within us,[41] and gives us the power to resist sin. We are no longer controlled by our sinful nature, but by the Holy Spirit.[42] Those who live in accordance with the Spirit have their minds set on what the Spirit desires.[43] In contrast, the sinful mind is hostile to God and does not submit to God's law.[44]

The mind controlled by the sinful nature is death, but the mind controlled by the Spirit is life and peace.[45] Things will go much

---

Their sins and lawless acts I will remember no more.
(Hebrews 10:17)[39]

As far as the east is from the west, so far has he removed our transgressions from us.
(Psalm 103:12)[40]

Repent and be baptized, every one of you, in the name of Jesus Christ for the forgiveness of your sins.
And you will receive the gift of the Holy Spirit.
(Acts 2:38)[41]

You [believers], are controlled not by the sinful nature but by the Spirit, if the Spirit of God lives in you.
(Romans 8:9)[42]

Those who live according to the sinful nature have their minds set on what that nature desires; but those who live in accordance with the Spirit have their minds set on what the Spirit desires.
(Romans 8:5)[43]

The sinful mind is hostile to God. It does not submit to God's law, nor can it do so. Those controlled by the sinful nature cannot please God.
(Romans 8:7-8)[44]

The mind of the sinful man is death, but the mind controlled by the Spirit is life and peace.
(Romans 8:6)[45]

better in this world if, through the help of the Holy Spirit, we resist evil[46] and do what is right.[47]

Unfortunately, in their struggle against sin, Christians sometimes lose the battle. They are by no means perfect.[48] They sometimes find themselves doing the very things they do not want to do.[49] But the important thing is that they do not give up. Throughout their lives, they try to be more and more Christ-like and avoid willfully sinning.[50]

In fact, if you are a Christian it would be a serious mistake to continue willfully sinning when you know what you are doing is morally wrong. God cannot be fooled. People who deliberately keep on sinning even when they know God's truth are in danger of being judged by God and receiving His wrath.[51]

> Resist the devil, and he will flee from you.
> **(James 4:7)**[46]

> This is what the Lord says: Do what is just and right.
> **(Jeremiah 22:3)**[47]

> Not that I have already obtained all this, or have already been made perfect, but I press on to take hold of that for which Christ Jesus took hold of me.
> **(Philippians 3:12)**[48]

> So I find this law at work: When I want to do good, evil is right there with me.
> **(Romans 7:21)**[49]

> Keep your servant also from willful sins; may they not rule over me. Then I will be blameless, innocent of great transgression.
> **(Psalm 19:13)**[50]

> If we deliberately keep on sinning after we have received the knowledge of the truth, no sacrifice for sins is left, but only a fearful expectation of judgment and of raging fire that will consume the enemies of God.
> **(Hebrews 10:26-27)**[51]

Ultimately, despite the best efforts of Christians to avoid sinning, they cannot totally overcome their inherent sinful nature;[52] as a result, all human beings, including Christians, experience a physical death.[53]

However, because of the redeeming love and sacrifice of Christ on the cross, Christians are raised from the dead and their sins are forgiven.[54] They are "set free" from sin, and they go to dwell in the house of the Lord for eternity.[55-57]

Now if I do what I do not want to do, it is no longer I who do it, but it is sin living in me that does it.
(Romans 7:20)[52]

For the wages of sin is death, but the gift of God is eternal life in Christ Jesus our Lord.
(Romans 6:23)[53]

In him we have redemption through his blood, the forgiveness of sins, in accordance with the riches of God's grace that he lavished on us with all wisdom and understanding.
(Ephesians 1:7-8)[54]

For Christ died for sins once for all, the righteous for the unrighteous, to bring you to God.
(1 Peter 3:18)[55]

He appeared so that he might take away our sins.
(1 John 3:5)[56]

"Look, the Lamb of God, who takes away the sin of the world!"
(John 1:29)[57]

Lesson 27

Suffering

"I consider that our present sufferings are not worth comparing with the glory that will be revealed in us."
(Romans 8:18)

Suffer: to feel pain or distress; sustain loss, injury, harm, or punishment

Physical pain and suffering are part of the human existence. No one likes to suffer, and it is difficult to understand why an all loving God would allow his children to experience pain, sickness, illness, handicaps, incurable diseases, and death. However, God did not create the world this way. It was only through man's disobedience and rebellion that suffering and death entered into the world.

Do not blame God. Instead, in your suffering turn to the Lord for healing, comfort, and help in dealing with your pain and afflictions. Suffering is not always "bad" for us. Suffering can bring us closer to God and point us toward the eternal glory that awaits us in heaven—where there will be no more pain and suffering, and where we will spend eternity with God.

Synopsis

When God first created man, physical pain, suffering, and death did not exist; it was only after Adam and Eve disobeyed God in the Garden of Eden (after being tempted by Satan) that suffering and death entered into the world. Satan, not God, is the original cause of physical and emotional suffering.

Once established, physical pain and suffering have preoccupied man's attention throughout the ages. From the Old Testament onward, God's people have cried out to Him in pain and suffering.[1,2]

I am in pain and distress; may your salvation, O God, protect me. **(Psalm 69:29)**[1]

Be merciful to me, LORD, for I am faint; O LORD, heal me, for my bones are in agony. **(Psalm 6:2)**[2]

On some occasions, God has directly answered their prayers and cries for help and at times miraculously healed them.[3-7] During His ministry on earth, Jesus performed many miracles and healed people who were blind, crippled, ill, or diseased.[8-11]

> Heal me, O Lord, and I will be healed; save me and I will be saved, for you are the one I praise.
> **(Jeremiah 17:14)**[3]

> O Lord my God, I called to you for help and you healed me.
> **(Psalm 30:2)**[4]

> For he will deliver the needy who cry out,
> the afflicted who have no one to help.
> **(Psalm 72:12)**[5]

> The Lord will sustain him on his sickbed and restore him from his bed of illness.
> **(Psalm 41:3)**[6]

> For he has not despised or disdained the suffering of the afflicted one; he has not hidden his face from him but has listened to his cry for help.
> **(Psalm 22:24)**[7]

> When the sun was setting, the people brought to Jesus all who had various kinds of sickness, and laying his hands on each one, he healed them.
> **(Luke 4:40)**[8]

> News about him spread all over Syria, and people brought to him all who were ill with various diseases, those suffering severe pain, the demon-possessed, those having seizures, and the paralyzed, and he healed him.
> **(Matthew 4:24)**[9]

> And the people tried to touch him, because power was coming from him and healing them all.
> **(Luke 6:19)**[10]

> The blind and the lame came to him at the temple, and he healed them.
> **(Matthew 21:14)**[11]

The same power and authority to heal physical illness was given to the original disciples of Christ.[12] Later on, following Christ's death on the cross, people in the early church who were sick were instructed to call on the elders to pray over them and anoint them with oil in the name of the Lord, in order to receive physical healing.[13]

However, despite the fact that God is able to miraculously heal us from all our infirmities, He does not always do so. Jesus Christ Himself endured pain and suffering when He walked on this earth; God did not spare Him from the anguish of the cross.[14,15]

In fact, physical pain, suffering, and afflictions can turn out to be extremely important and beneficial to our spiritual growth.[16] As we look back over our lives, we may even be glad that we suffered because of all the benefits we have reaped.[17]

> He called his twelve disciples to him and gave them authority to drive out evil spirits and to heal every disease and sickness.
> **(Matthew 10:1)**[12]

> Is any one of you sick? He should call the elders of the church to pray over him and anoint him with oil in the name of the Lord. And the prayer offered in faith will make the sick person well; the Lord will raise him up.
> **(James 5:14-15)**[13]

> He was despised and rejected by men,
> a man of sorrows, and familiar with suffering.
> **(Isaiah 53:3)**[14]

> But he was pierced for our transgressions,
> he was crushed for our iniquities...and by his wounds we are healed.
> **(Isaiah 53:5)**[15]

> Surely it was for my benefit that I suffered such anguish.
> **(Isaiah 38:17)**[16]

> Make us glad for as many days as you have afflicted us,
> for as many years as we have seen trouble.
> **(Psalm 90:15)**[17]

> It was good for me to be afflicted
> so that I might learn your decrees.
> **(Psalm 119:71)**[18]

Suffering helps us by encouraging us to turn to God's Word and His promises as contained in the Bible.[18,19] Through suffering, we learn to trust and obey God even in the midst of our afflictions.[20] If we turn to Him, we find that God often speaks most clearly to us during times of suffering.[21]

Suffering can help build important personality traits, such as perseverance, character, and hope.[22] In our suffering and brokenness, as we turn our thoughts toward God's Word and toward heaven and eternity, our minds are renewed and we no longer focus on earthly pleasures and sinful ways.[23,24]

Through suffering, we develop a deeper perspective on life and we begin to understand that our "momentary" suffering here on earth does not compare to the eternal glory that awaits us in heaven.[25] It

> Look upon my suffering and deliver me,
> for I have not forgotten your law.
> **(Psalm 119:153)**[19]
>
> Before I was afflicted I went astray,
> but now I obey your word.
> **(Psalm 119:67)**[20]
>
> But those who suffer he delivers in their suffering;
> he speaks to them in their affliction.
> **(Job 36:15)**[21]
>
> We also rejoice in our sufferings, because we know that suffering produces perseverance; perseverance, character; and character, hope.
> **(Romans 5:3-4)**[22]
>
> Therefore, since Christ suffered in his body, arm yourselves also with the same attitude, because he who has suffered in his body is done with sin.
> **(1 Peter 4:1)**[23]
>
> As a result [of suffering] he does not live the rest of his earthly life for evil human desires, but rather for the will of God.
> **(1 Peter 4:2)**[24]
>
> I consider that our present sufferings are not worth comparing with the glory that will be revealed in us.
> **(Romans 8:18)**[25]

is the backdrop of eternity that helps make our earthly pain and suffering tolerable.[26-28]

God does not promise us a "painless" or trouble free world; but He does promise us that He has overcome this world.[29] When Christ returns, things will be radically changed. There will no longer be pain or suffering and God will wipe away our tears.[30] It is difficult to imagine what God has prepared for us, but we know it is going to be *beyond our wildest dreams or imagination.*[31,32] Praise be to God![33]

The body that is sown is perishable, it is raised imperishable;
it is sown in dishonor, it is raised in glory; it is sown in weakness,
it is raised in power; it is sown a natural body,
it is raised a spiritual body.
(1 Corinthians 15:42-44)[26]

They will enter Zion with singing; everlasting joy will crown
their heads. Gladness and joy will overtake them,
and sorrow and sighing will flee away.
(Isaiah 35:10)[27]

And the God of all grace, who called you to his eternal glory in
Christ, after you have suffered a little while, will himself restore
you and make you strong, firm and steadfast.
(1 Peter 5:10)[28]

*In this world you will have trouble. But take heart!
I have overcome the world.*
(John 16:33)[29]

He will wipe every tear from their eyes. There will be no more
death or mourning or crying or pain, for the old order of
things has passed away.
(Revelation 21:4)[30]

No eye has seen, no ear has heard, no mind has conceived what
God has prepared for those who love him.
(1 Corinthians 2:9)[31]

He has made everything beautiful in its time. He has also set
eternity in the hearts of men; yet they cannot fathom what
God has done from beginning to end.
(Ecclesiastes 3:11)[32]

To him be the power for ever and ever. Amen.
(1 Peter 5:11)[33]

God's Guidance

Some people mistakenly believe that all suffering is a result of sin. However, Jesus Himself dispelled this notion when He healed a man who was blind from birth. His disciples asked Jesus, "Rabbi, who sinned, this man or his parents, that he was born blind?" Jesus answered, *"Neither this man nor his parents sinned,"* said Jesus, *"but this happened so that the work of God might be displayed in his life."* (John 9:1-3)

We do not always have an explanation for the pain and suffering that we experience in this world. If you or your loved ones are suffering, do not lose hope.[34-36] Turn to God for help, comfort, and strength.[37-45]

Find rest, O my soul, in God alone; my hope comes from him.
(Psalm 62:5)[34]

Anyone who is among the living has hope.
(Ecclesiastes 9:4)[35]

Why are you downcast, O my soul? Why so disturbed within me? Put your hope in God, for I will yet praise him, my Savior and my God.
(Psalm 42:5)[36]

Therefore we do not lose heart. Though outwardly we are wasting away, yet inwardly we are being renewed day by day.
(2 Corinthians 4:16)[37]

Praise be to the Lord, to God our Savior,
who daily bears our burdens.
(Psalm 68:19)[38]

Surely he took up our infirmities and carried our sorrows.
(Isaiah 53:4)[39]

Sustain me according to your promise, and I will live;
do not let my hopes be dashed.
(Psalm 119:116)[40]

For just as the sufferings of Christ flow over into our lives, so also through Christ our comfort overflows.
(2 Corinthians 1:5)[41]

I, even I, am he who comforts you.
(Isaiah 51:12)[42]

Turn to God's Word for encouragement through the Scriptures.[46,47]
Cast all your anxiety on Him because he cares for you.[48]

Finally, as Christians, the act of helping others who are suffering is one of the most Christ-like things we can do.[49-53]

For the LORD comforts his people
and will have compassion on his afflicted ones.
(Isaiah 49:13)[43]

He gives strength to the weary,
and increases the power of the weak.
(Isaiah 40:29)[44]

*Come to me, all you who are weary and burdened,
and I will give you rest.*
(Matthew 11:28)[45]

For everything that was written in the past was written to
teach us, so that through endurance and the encouragement
of the Scriptures we might have hope.
(Romans 15:4)[46]

My soul is weary with sorrow;
strengthen me according to your word.
(Psalm 119:28)[47]

Cast all your anxiety on him because he cares for you.
(1 Peter 5:7)[48]

Love one another deeply, form the heart.
(1 Peter 1:22)[49]

Carry each other's burdens,
and in this way you will fulfill the law of Christ.
(Galatians 6:2)[50]

Be devoted to one another in brotherly love.
(Romans 12:10)[51]

The only thing that counts is faith expressing itself through love.
(Galatians 5:6)[52]

*So in everything, do to others what you would have them
do to you, for this sums up the Law and the Prophets.*
(Matthew 6:12)[53]

Lesson 28

Temptation

"But when you are tempted, he will also provide a way out so that you can stand up under it."
(1 Corinthians 10:13)

Temptation: an enticement or solicitation to sin

The devil is the original source of temptation in our world. From the time he first tempted Adam and Eve to eat of the forbidden fruit, he has been working to draw men into sin. Fortunately for mankind, God sent His son, Jesus Christ, to save humanity from sin and to defeat the work of the devil. If we turn to God for help and follow the advice given in the Bible, we can resist temptation and keep from sinning.

Synopsis

The following is the story of how temptation entered into the world and how it will ultimately be defeated.

Lucifer (later renamed "devil" and "Satan") was a powerful angel who was banished from heaven because he desired to be equal to God. After falling out of favor with God, he came to earth and appears in the story of Adam and Eve. Satan took the form of a serpent (Rev.12:9) and tempted Eve to eat of the forbidden fruit (that gave knowledge of good and evil). He deceived her and told her that if she ate the fruit she would be like God.

Eve ate of the forbidden fruit, and then gave it to Adam to eat. When God saw what they had done, he was angered by their actions and expelled them from the Garden of Eden. Because of "Adam's fall" (that is, his disobedience), all human beings have inherited a sinful nature.

During the years following the lives of Adam and Eve, the world fell deeper and deeper into sin because of the work of Satan on earth. In response to the ever-increasing sin, God sent His only son, Jesus Christ, to save mankind from sin and defeat the work of the evil one (ie, the devil).[1]

When fulfilling this mission, Christ Himself was tempted by the devil,[2] but He did not give in to sin. Following His temptation in the wilderness, Jesus experienced first-hand just how potentially powerful Satan could be.[3] As a result, He prayed to God that His Heavenly Father would protect His disciples from the influence of the devil.[4] In a similar fashion, when He taught His followers how to pray (the famous "Lord's Prayer"), He taught them to pray to God to deliver them from temptation and from the evil one.[5]

As we consider the work of the devil, remember that his main objective is to tempt human beings to sin and disobey God. In order to achieve this objective, the devil is incredibly "tricky" and resourceful. He is a liar[6] and a murderer[7] and he never tells the truth.[7] He is a master of deception, and he pretends to be good

---

The reason the Son of God appeared
was to destroy the devil's work.
(1 John 3:8)[1]

Then Jesus was led by the Spirit into the desert
to be tempted by the devil.
(Matthew 4:1)[2]

For we do not have a high priest who is unable to sympathize
with our weaknesses, but we have one who has been tempted
in every way, just as we are—yet was without sin.
(Hebrews 5:15)[3]

*My prayer is not that you take them out of the world
but that you protect them from the evil one.*
(John 17:15)[4]

And lead us not into temptation, but deliver us from the evil one.
(Matthew 6:13)[5]

*When he lies, he speaks his native language,
for he is a liar and the father of lies.*
(John 8:44)[6]

*He was a murderer from the beginning, not holding to the truth,
for there is no truth in him.*
(John 8:44)[7]

when in fact he is not.⁸ He is aware of our weaknesses, and he is always lurking in the background of our lives, scheming and plotting and waiting for a chance to entice us into sin.⁹

Even more disturbing, the Bible tells us that Satan does not work alone.¹⁰ Other evil spirits also do his work.** But despite the relentless efforts of Satan and his followers, it is important to understand that, when all is said and done, God wins!

Although the non-Christian world is hopelessly under the control of Satan, Christians are not alone in their struggles.¹¹ Satan is not more powerful than the Holy Spirit who dwells within each and every Christian.¹² And Satan cannot bring eternal harm to God's children. The Lord strengthens and protects us from the devil¹³ and limits his power over us.

> Satan himself masquerades as an angel of light.
> **(2 Corinthians 11:14)**⁸
>
> Your enemy the devil prowls around like a roaring lion looking for someone to devour.
> **(1 Peter 5:8)**⁹
>
> Dear friends, do not believe every spirit, but test the spirits to see whether they are from God.
> **(1 John 4:1)**¹⁰
>
> We know that we are children of God, and that the whole world is under the control of the evil one.
> **(1 John 5:19)**¹¹
>
> The one who is in you [the Holy Spirit] is greater than the one who is in the world.
> **(1 John 4:4)**¹²
>
> But the Lord is faithful, and he will strengthen and protect you from the evil one.
> **(2 Thessalonians 3:3)**¹³

**For example, evil spirits sometimes attempt to deceive God's people by leading them to think that the Holy Spirit is inspiring the message given by a teacher or preacher when in fact it is being inspired by the lying spirit of the devil. The way to discern the difference is to test whether the spirit acknowledges Jesus Christ as the Son of God. (1 John 4:22-3)

Although all human beings are tempted by the devil to do evil, God will never let you be tempted beyond what you can bear,[14] and He will always provide a way out so that you can achieve victory over the temptation.[15,16]

Therefore, you should never blame God if you "give in" to temptation and sin. In the face of temptation, you have a choice. The final decision to sin or not to sin is your own.

And you should not blame God for the fact that you are being tempted in the first place. God Himself does not tempt human beings.[17] It is the work of the devil and our own evil desires that lead us into temptation.[17]

In the end, when Christ once again returns to earth, the devil will finally be silenced. There will be a day when he is no longer able to tempt us to sin. God will eventually crush Satan[18] and drive him out of this world.[19] He will be judged by God and thrown into hell, where he will be tortured day and night for ever and ever.[20]

> And God is faithful; he will not let you be tempted
> beyond what you can bear.
> **(1 Corinthians 10:13)**[14]
>
> But when you are tempted, he will also provide a way out
> so that you can stand up under it.
> **(1 Corinthians 10:13)**[15]
>
> The Lord knows how to rescue godly men from trials.
> **(2 Peter 2:9)**[16]
>
> When tempted, no one should say, "God is tempting me."
> For God cannot be tempted by evil, nor does he tempt anyone;
> but each one is tempted when, by his own evil desire,
> he is dragged away and enticed.
> **(James 1:13-14)**[17]
>
> The God of peace will soon crush Satan under your feet.
> **(Romans 16:20)**[18]
>
> *Now is the time for judgment on this world; now the prince of this world will be driven out.* **(John 12:31)**[19]
>
> And the devil, who deceived them, was thrown into the lake of burning sulfur, where the beast and the false prophet had been thrown. They will be tormented day and night for ever and ever.
> **(Revelation 20:10)**[20]

God's Guidance

How can temptation be overcome?

Stay Alert and Keep Your Guard Up: One of the best ways to protect yourself from temptation is to stay alert and keep your guard up.[21-23] You may think that you are spiritually strong and able to withstand temptation, but remember that the flesh is weak.[21]

If you have an area of sin in your life where you are particularly vulnerable to sin, you should be vigilant and pay special attention to that area so that the temptation does not "sneak through" your defenses and lead you to sin.

Test everything that comes into your senses and determine whether it is of God or of the evil one. Hold on to what is good, and avoid that which is evil.[24]

Avoid "Dangerous" Situations: Learn to avoid situations that are likely to lead to the temptation to sin. For example, if you are married, don't deprive each other of normal sexual relations, or you will expose yourself to the obvious temptation of Satan.[25]

Watch and pray so that you will not fall into temptation.
The spirit is willing, but the body is weak.
(Matthew 25:26)[21]

Be self-controlled and alert.
(1 Peter 5:8)[22]

In the paths of the wicked lie thorns and snares,
but he who guards his soul stays far from them.
(Proverbs 22:5)[23]

Test everything. Hold on to the good. Avoid every kind of evil.
(1 Thessalonians 5:21-22)[24]

Do not deprive each other except by mutual consent and for a time, so that you may devote yourselves to prayer. Then come together again so that Satan will not tempt you because of your lack of self-control.
(1 Corinthians 7:5)[25]

Don't let the sun go down while you are still angry, or you might give the devil a foothold, which will result in sin.[26] And don't run around trying to get rich, for such people often fall into temptation and a trap, which ultimately plunges them into ruin and destruction.[27]

Put on the Armor of God: One of the most important things you can do to resist temptation[28] is to put on the "full armor of God" so that you can defend yourself against the devil's schemes.[29] To understand this analogy, think of a Roman soldier ready for battle. Each part of the uniform represents a part of the spiritual armor that you should be wearing in order to protect yourself from the evil one.

The **belt** of the uniform represents "truth."[30] When battling the devil, it always important to focus on the truth,[31] since we have already seen that the evil one "lies and deceives." Jesus Christ

---

Do not let the sun go down while you are still angry,
and do not give the devil a foothold.
(Ephesians 4:26-27)[26]

People who want to get rich fall into temptation and a trap
and into many foolish and harmful desires that plunge
men into ruin and destruction.
(1 Timothy 6:9)[27]

Resist the devil, and he will flee from you.
(James 4:7)[28]

Put on the full armor of God so that you can take your stand
against the devil's schemes.
(Ephesians 6:11)[29]

Stand firm then, with the belt of truth buckled around
your waist, with the breastplate of righteousness in place,
and with your feet fitted with the readiness that comes
from the gospel of peace.
(Ephesians 6:14-15)[30]

Surely you desire truth in the inner parts;
you teach me wisdom in the inmost place.
(Psalm 51:6)[31]

proclaimed that He was the "way and the truth and the life."[32] If we follow Christ's teachings, then we will know the truth and the truth will set us free from the influence of the devil.[33]

We can also find truth by becoming sensitive to the Holy Spirit, who is sometimes called the "Spirit of truth."[34] When we first accept Christ as our Lord and Savior, the Holy Spirit comes to reside in us. This is how we know that we are children of God.[35] The Holy Spirit is the great Counselor who was sent by God to guide us into all truth.[36] We need to listen to the Holy Spirit and not "grieve the Holy Spirit" by sinning and falling prey to the temptation of the evil one.[37]

The **breastplate** of the uniform represents "righteousness." The more righteous and holy you are, the better prepared you will be to resist the temptation of the evil one. You are to conduct yourself in a manner that is worthy of the gospel of Christ.[38] At the end of

---

I am the way and the truth and the life. No one comes to the Father except through me.
(John 14:6)[32]

If you hold to my teaching, you are really my disciples. Then you will know the truth, and the truth will set you free.
(John 8:31-32)[33]

But when he, the Spirit of truth, comes, he will guide you into all truth.
(John 16:13)[34]

And this is how we know that he lives in us: We know it by the Spirit he gave us.
(1 John 3:24)[35]

When the Counselor comes, whom I will send to you from the Father, the Spirit of truth who goes out from the Father, he will testify about me.
(John 15:26)[36]

And do not grieve the Holy Spirit of God, with whom you were sealed for the day of redemption.
(Ephesians 4:30)[37]

Whatever happens, conduct yourselves in a manner worthy of the gospel of Christ.
(Philippians 1:27)[38]

the day, if you stay the course, your righteousness will "shine like the sun in the kingdom of God."[39]

The **shoes** the soldier is wearing represent your readiness to spread the "gospel of peace."[40] The more willing and ready you are to go out into the world and preach the gospel of Christ,[40] the more peace you will have within yourself,[41] and the better prepared you will be to resist the devil.

The **shield** the soldier uses represents "faith."[42] Take time to develop your faith and belief in Jesus Christ, so that the strength of your faith will stand fast against the attack of the evil one.[43-45]

The **helmet** of the uniform represents "salvation."[46] Remember the price that Christ paid on the cross (when He suffered an agonizing

---

Then the righteous will shine like the sun in the kingdom of their Father. He who has ears, let him hear.
(Matthew 13:43)[39]

He came and preached peace to you who were far away and peace to those who were near.
(Ephesians 2:17)[40]

I have told you these things, so that in me you may have peace.
(John 16:33)[41]

In addition to all this, take up the shield of faith, with which you can extinguish all the flaming arrows of the evil one.
(Ephesians 6:16)[42]

Now faith is being sure of what we hope for and certain of what we do not see.
(Hebrews 11:1)[43]

Build yourselves up in your most holy faith and pray in the Holy Spirit.
(Jude 1:20)[44]

Fight the good fight of the faith.
(1 Timothy 6:12)[45]

Take the helmet of salvation and the sword of the Spirit, which is the word of God.
(Ephesians 6:17)[46]

death and died for your sins)[47,48] so that you could live with Him forever in heaven. The devil may try to trick you into thinking that you aren't saved, or that the sin in which he is trying to get you to engage "isn't that important." Remember that our Savior does not want you to sin, and that He suffered and died for each and every sin you choose to commit.[49,50]

Finally, the **sword** of the uniform represents the "Word of God." One of the best defenses against the devil's temptation is for you to hide the Word of God in your heart so that you do not sin against the Lord.[51,52] Every word of God is perfect[53] and flawless[54] and it will stand forever.[55] Do not neglect God's Word,[56] for it will make you wiser than all your enemies, including the devil.[57]

> You were bought at a price; do not become slaves of men.
> **(1 Corinthians 7:23)**[47]
>
> At just the right time, when were still powerless,
> Christ died for the ungodly.
> **(Romans 5:6)**[48]
>
> He was delivered over to death for our sins
> and was raised to life for our justification.
> **(Romans 4:25)**[49]
>
> This is love: not that we loved God, but that he loved us
> and sent his Son as an atoning sacrifice for our sins.
> **(1 John 4:10)**[50]
>
> I have hidden your word in my heart
> that I might not sin against you.
> **(Psalm 119:11)**[51]
>
> When your words came, I ate them; they were my joy and my heart's delight, for I bear your name, O Lord God Almighty.
> **(Jeremiah 15:16)**[52]
>
> The law of the Lord is perfect, reviving the soul.
> **(Psalm 19:7)**[53]
>
> Every word of God is flawless.
> **(Proverbs 30:5)**[54]
>
> The grass withers and the flowers fall,
> but the word of our God stands forever.
> **(Isaiah 40:8)**[55]

Prayer: We have already discussed the importance of prayer in overcoming temptation. By way of review, remember that when you are confronted with temptation, if you turn to God, He will always give you a "way out,"[15,16] and God will never let you be tempted beyond what you can bear.[14]

Humbly submit **your will** to **God's will**, and pray for His strength and guidance. You may not be able to fight the temptation on your own, but it is certainly not too big for God.

I will not neglect your word.
(Psalm 119:16)[56]

Your commands make me wiser than my enemies,
for they are ever with me.
(Psalm 119:98)[57]

Lesson 29

Thinking, Healthy

"Take captive every thought to make it
obedient to Christ."
(2 Corinthians 10:5)

Thinking: mental processing;
evaluating and reasoning

Our thinking is greatly influenced by our underlying beliefs. We have a choice. We can either believe the lies taught by the world (and the devil), or believe the truths taught in the Bible, and as manifested in the perfect life of Jesus Christ.

As Christians, God expects us to bring our thinking into line with the truth (See Lesson 29). He pays close attention to our thinking. We cannot hide our thoughts from God.

Importantly, God has provided us with free will, and the tools and means by which we can begin to change our thought life: by diligently studying the truth as revealed in the Holy Bible; by focusing our thoughts on the life and teachings of Jesus; and by praying for guidance from the Holy Spirit (the Spirit of truth). In the end, our thinking is transformed in remarkable and wonderful ways, as we become more and more Christ-like.

Synopsis

God is deeply concerned about our thinking.[1] We cannot hide our thoughts from God.[2] He is aware of everything we are thinking and knows what we are going to say before we speak.[3]

I the LORD search the heart and examine the mind.
(Jeremiah 17:10)[1]

Yet you know me, O LORD; you see me and test
my thoughts about you.
(Jeremiah 12:3)[2]

Before a word is on my tongue you know it completely, O LORD.
(Psalm 139:4) [3]

God detests the thoughts of the wicked, but is pleased with thoughts of the pure in heart.[4] Each and every thought we have, whether good or bad, is judged by the standard of God's Word, as contained in the Holy Bible.[5]

As Christians, we are born with a sinful nature,[6] but God has given us the free will to focus our minds on evil, or focus our thoughts on God and truth.

The sinful mind is hostile to God, and does not submit to His law.[7] Those who live according to their sinful nature have their minds focused on what their sinful nature desires. On the other hand, those who live according to the Spirit have their minds focused on what the Spirit desires.[8]

The mind of the sinful man leads to death, but the mind controlled by the Spirit leads to life and peace.[9] If we are Spirit filled and focus on God's Word, we will truly have the mind of Christ.[10]

The LORD detests the thoughts of the wicked, but those of the pure are pleasing to him. **(Proverbs 15:26)**[4]

For the word of God is living and active. Sharper than any double-edged sword, it penetrates even to dividing soul and spirit, joints and marrow; it judges the thoughts and attitudes of the heart. **(Hebrews 4:12)**[5]

Surely I was sinful from at birth, sinful from the time my mother conceived me. **(Psalm 51:5)**[6]

The sinful mind is hostile to God. It does not submit to God's law, nor can it do so. Those controlled by the sinful nature cannot please God. **(Romans 8:7-8)**[7]

Those who live according to the sinful nature have their minds set on what that nature desires; but those who live in accordance with the Spirit have their minds set on what the Spirit desires.
(Romans 8:5)[8]

The mind of sinful man is death, but the mind controlled by the Spirit is life and peace. **(Romans 8:6)**[9]

But we have the mind of Christ.
(1 Corinthians 2:16)[10]

Fortunately, God provides a great deal of advice about how we, as Christians, can take control of our thinking and make it pleasing to Him.

God's Guidance

First of all, we are to monitor our thoughts and reject and demolish any thoughts that run contrary to God's truth; we are to take captive every thought and make it obedient to Christ.[11] We are to work to get control over our thinking and stop thinking in immature, childish ways.[12,13]

We are to stop dwelling on the past and on things we can't change.[14] We are to focus our thoughts on positive aspects of our lives rather than on the negative—that is, we are to think about whatever is: true, noble, right, pure, lovely, admirable, excellent or praiseworthy.[15]

We demolish arguments and every pretension that sets itself up against the knowledge of God, and we take captive every thought to make it obedient to Christ.
(2 Corinthians 10:5)[11]

When I was a child, I talked like a child, I thought like a child, I reasoned like a child. When I became a man, I put childish ways behind me.
(1 Corinthians 13:11)[12]

Brothers, stop thinking like children. In regard to evil be infants, but in your thinking be adults.
(1 Corinthians 14:20)[13]

Brothers, I do not consider myself yet to have taken hold of it. But one thing I do: Forgetting what is behind and straining toward what is ahead, I press on toward the goal to win the prize for which God has called me heavenward in Christ Jesus.
(Philippians 3:13-14)[14]

Finally, brothers, whatever is true, whatever is noble, whatever is right, whatever is pure, whatever is lovely, whatever is admirable—if anything is excellent or praiseworthy—think about such things.
(Philippians 4:8)[15]

We are to stop thinking as the world thinks, and no longer conform to the pattern of thought that is prevalent in our society.[16]

We are to strive to keep our conscience clear before God.[17] We are to focus our minds on the truth as revealed by the Holy Spirit,[18] and fix our thoughts on Jesus,[19] the author and perfecter of our faith.[20]

When we get our thinking straight and aligned with the spiritual truths, healthy emotions naturally follow. For example, the fruits of the Spirit are: love, joy, peace, patience, kindness, goodness, faithfulness, gentleness and self-control.[21]

In contrast, if we believe in the lies and the irrational beliefs taught by the world (and by the devil), we will experience negative emotions such as anger (Lesson 4), anxiety (Lesson 5), and depression (Lesson 12). The Bible abounds with information on how to avoid experiencing these emotions by focusing on the truth, as revealed in the Scriptures.

Do not conform any longer to the pattern of this world, but be transformed by the renewing of your mind. Then you will be able to test and approve what God's will is—his good, pleasing and perfect will.
(Romans 12:2)[16]

So I strive always to keep my conscience clear before God and man.
(Acts 24:16)[17]

But when he, the Spirit of truth, comes, he will guide you into all truth.
(John 16:13)[18]

Therefore, holy brothers, who share in the heavenly calling, fix your thoughts on Jesus, the apostle and high priest whom we confess.
(Hebrews 3:1)[19]

Let us fix our eyes on Jesus, the author and perfector of our faith.
(Hebrews 12:2)[20]

But the fruit of the Spirit is love, joy, peace, kindness, faithfulness, gentleness, and self-control.
(Galatians 5:22-23)[21]

Finally, our underlying beliefs (and the thinking that flows from our beliefs), can have a profound influence on our behavior—that is, the actions we take as Christians. God does not want us to simply hear the word and believe; He wants us to put our beliefs into practice.[22]

The Scriptures tell us that faith without action is dead.[23] It is not enough to talk about our faith to others;[24] God requires us to live out our faith in our own behavior and in our actions toward our fellow man.[25-27]

One of the greatest testimonies of our faith in action is our love for others. As we come to accept and obey the truth of the Bible and start to live out the truth in our thinking and in our behavior, we will naturally start to love one another deeply, from the heart.[28]

My mother and brothers are those who hear God's word and put it into practice.
(Luke 8:21)[22]

As the body without the spirit is dead,
so faith without deed is dead.
(James 2:26)[23]

Dear children, let us not love with words or tongue
but with actions and in truth.
(1 John 3:18)[24]

A person is justified by what he does and not by faith alone.
(James 2:24)[25]

Now that you know these things,
you will be blessed if you do them.
(John 13:17)[26]

Do not merely listen to the word, and so deceive yourselves.
Do what it says.
(James 1:22)[27]

Now that you have purified yourselves by obeying the truth
so that you have sincere love for your brothers, love one
another deeply, from the heart.
(1 Peter 1:22)[28]

Lesson 30

Trouble/Hardship

"In this world you will have trouble."
(John 16:33)

Trouble: a state of distress, affliction, difficulty, or need

We live in a world that is full of troubles. It seems that everywhere we turn, there are problems and difficulties that cause us unrest. Widespread poverty, natural disasters, and hardships of many kinds are common in our modern society. However, in many ways, our current situation is no different than it was when Jesus walked this earth. If you are in trouble, turn to the Bible for help and guidance.

Synopsis

God does not promise a trouble-free world; in fact we should expect to have problems and hardships during our time on this earth.[1] Sometimes our troubles are a direct result of our own actions and our own sin.[2] However, this is not always the case. The Bible reminds us that even righteous men experience troubles and hardships,[3] and that we all will have days filled with light and sun, and days filled with darkness.[4]

In this world you will have trouble.
(John 16:33)[1]

There will be trouble and distress
for every human being who does evil.
(Romans 2:9)[2]

A righteous man may have many troubles,
but the Lord delivers him from them all.
(Psalm 34:19)[3]

Some people are forced to live in poverty. Although the poor and needy may feel that the Lord has forgotten them—He has not.[5] He will take pity on the weak and needy,[6] and He will be their refuge.[7] As Christians, we are to defend the rights of the poor and needy,[8] and speak up for those who are destitute and who cannot speak for themselves.[9]

Other people experience natural disasters and lose most or all of their material possessions. Even in this situation, God does not want us to fear.[10,11] If we call on Him, He will answer us in our distress.[12] We can take refuge in Him.[13]

Light is sweet, and it pleases the eyes to see the sun. However many years a man may live, let him enjoy them all. But let him remember the days of darkness, for they will be many.
(Ecclesiastes 11:7-8)[4]

The needy will not always be forgotten,
nor the hope of the afflicted ever perish.
(Psalm 9:18)[5]

He will take pity on the weak and the needy
and save the needy from death.
(Psalm 72:13)[6]

You have been a refuge for the poor, a refuge for the needy in his distress, a shelter from the storm and a shade from the heat.
(Isaiah 25:4)[7]

Defend the rights of the poor and needy.
(Proverbs 31:9)[8]

Speak up for those who cannot speak for themselves,
for the rights of all who are destitute.
(Proverbs 31:8)[9]

Have no fear of sudden disaster or of the ruin that overtakes the wicked, for the LORD will be your confidence and will keep your foot from being snared.
(Proverbs 3:25)[10]

In God I trust; I will not be afraid. What can man do to me?
(Psalm 56:11)[11]

I call on the LORD in my distress, and he answers me.
(Psalm 120:1)[12]

As human beings, there is a tendency to think of all troubles as being "bad." However, God's Word reveals that this is not always the case. Sometimes troubles and hardships can serve as "tests of our faith," and can result in glory and honor to God, as Jesus Christ is revealed in us.[14] At other times, hardships are a form of discipline that God allows us to experience because He loves us.[15]

Regardless of the source of our troubles, Christians who are following God's will are urged to look at all problems and hardships from a "positive" perspective. That is, God urges us to be joyful and thankful in all circumstances, regardless of what happens to us.[16]

God's Guidance

The most important thing you can do when you are in trouble is to pray.[17] Take time to pour out your heart to God and tell Him all of

> I will take refuge in the shadow of your wings
> until the disaster has passed.
> **(Psalm 57:1)**[13]

> In this you greatly rejoice, though now for a little while you
> may have had to suffer grief in all kinds of trials. These
> have come so that your faith—of greater worth than
> gold, which perishes even though refined by fire—may
> be proved genuine and may result in praise,
> glory and honor when Jesus Christ is revealed.
> **(1 Peter 1:6-7)**[14]

> Endure hardship as discipline; God is treating you as sons.
> For what son is not disciplined by his father?
> **(Hebrews 12:7)**[15]

> Be joyful always; pray continually; give thanks in all
> circumstances, for this is God's will for you in Christ Jesus.
> **(1 Thessalonians 5:16-18)**[16]

> Is any one of you in trouble? He should pray.
> **(James 5:13)**[17]

your troubles.[18] When we do this, God is always there to help.[19] He will provide refuge, strength,[20] and comfort.[21,22]

If you are in trouble, don't be afraid.[23] Your problems are not too big for the creator of the universe. God has overcome all of the world's problems and troubles.[24]

Finally, instead of focusing exclusively on your own troubles, try reaching out to others. Tell them about God and the comfort they can receive if they turn to Him.[25]

I pour out my complaint before him;
before him I tell my trouble.
(Psalm 142:2)[18]

Then you will call, and the LORD will answer;
you will cry for help, and he will say: Here am I.
(Isaiah 58:9)[19]

God is our refuge and strength,
an ever-present help in trouble.
(Psalm 46:1)[20]

For the LORD comforts his people and will have compassion
on his afflicted ones.
(Isaiah 49:13)[21]

Praise be to the God and Father of our Lord Jesus Christ,
the Father of compassion and the God of all comfort.
(2 Corinthians 1:3)[22]

Do not let your hearts be troubled and do not be afraid.
(James 14:27)[23]

*In this world you will have trouble. But take heart!
I have overcome the world.*
(John 16:33)[24]

Who comforts us in all our troubles, so that we can comfort
those in any trouble with the comfort we ourselves
have received from God.
(2 Corinthians 1:4)[25]

Lesson 31

Truth, Seeking

"I have chosen the way of truth;
I have set my heart on your laws."
(Psalm 119:30)

Truth: that which is accurate with respect to reality

The Bible is the only reliable source of truth for all mankind. It contains the infallible Word of God and the story of our Lord and Savior, Jesus Christ. God wants every human being to come to a knowledge of the truth and to be saved. The first (and by far the most important) truth to be grasped is that Jesus Christ, the Son of God, died for our sins so that we might receive eternal life. All other truths in the Bible hinge on this central truth.

As Christians, we are to seek truth and live our lives according to God's Word, and after the example of Jesus Christ.

Synopsis

God sent the truth in the form of His son, Jesus Christ.[1] Jesus Himself proclaimed: "I am the way, the truth, and the life."[2] God

---

We have seen his glory, the glory of the One and Only, who came from the Father, full of grace and truth.
(John 1:14)[1]

*I am the way and the truth and the life.
No one comes to the Father except through me.*
(John 14:6)[2]

our Savior wants all men to be saved and to come to a knowledge of the truth.[3,4]

If you are a believer, it is important to understand that God chose to give you birth through the word of truth; you are the "first-fruits" of all He created.[5] You were chosen by God from the beginning of time to be saved through the sanctifying work of the Holy Spirit and through belief in the truth.[6]

Throughout the lives of all individuals, God examines us to see if we are walking in the truth.[7] His desire is that His truth penetrates deep within us, to the core of our very being.[8]

In contrast, it is the devil's plan that we believe lies, for he is a liar and the father of lies; there is no truth in him.[9,10] We can protect

---

God our Savior...who wants all men to be saved
and come to a knowledge of the truth.
(1 Timothy 2:3-4)[3]

In fact, for this reason I was born, and for this I came into the world, to testify to the truth. Everyone on the side of truth listens to me.
(John 18:37)[4]

He chose to give us birth through the word of truth, that we might be a kind of first-fruits of all he created.
(James 1:18)[5]

From the beginning God chose you to be saved through the sanctifying work of the Spirit and through belief in the truth.
(2 Thessalonians 2:13)[6]

O Lord, do not your eyes look for truth?
(Jeremiah 5:3)[7]

Surely you desire truth in the inner parts; you teach me wisdom in the inmost place.
(Psalm 51:6)[8]

He [the devil] was a murderer from the beginning, not holding to the truth, for there is no truth in him.
(John 8:44)[9]

When he [the devil] lies, he speaks his native language, for he is a liar and the father of lies.
(John 8:44)[10]

ourselves from the lies of the devil by living in God's truth and abiding in God's love.[11]

The Bible is the main source of truth for mankind. It contains the Word of God and the teachings of his Son, Jesus Christ. Every word in the Bible is flawless,[12] perfect,[13] righteous,[14] trustworthy,[14] true[15] and eternal.[16]

As we study the Word of God we gain wisdom and understanding and ultimately, we start to "walk in the truth."[17] That is, as we learn God's commandments and start following them, our thinking and actions become more and more pure.[18] We are transformed and "born again" through the living and enduring Word of God that stands forever.[19] The final result of this process is that the truth literally "sets us free."[20]

> May your love and your truth always protect me.
> **(Psalm 40:11)**[11]
>
> Every word of God is flawless.
> **(Proverbs 30:5)**[12]
>
> The law of the LORD is perfect, reviving the soul.
> **(Psalm 19:7)**[13]
>
> The statutes you have laid down are righteous;
> they are fully trustworthy.
> **(Psalm 119:138)**[14]
>
> *Sanctify them by the truth; your word is truth.*
> **(John 17:17)**[15]
>
> All your words are true; all your righteous laws are eternal.
> **(Psalm 119:160)**[16]
>
> Test me, O LORD, and try me, examine my heart and my mind; for your love is ever before me, and I walk continually in your truth.
> **(Psalm 26:2)**[17]
>
> Now that you have purified yourselves by obeying the truth...
> love one another deeply, from the heart.
> **(1 Peter 1:22)**[18]
>
> For you have been born again, not of perishable seed, but of imperishable, through the living and enduring word of God.
> **(1 Peter 1:23)**[19]

In order for this transformation to take place, it is first necessary to accept and believe in the central truth of the Bible—that Jesus Christ (the Son of God) came to this earth to die for our sins[21] and that if we believe in Him and repent of our sins, we will inherit eternal life.[22] Once we accept this "gospel of salvation," we receive the Holy Spirit, who lives and dwells within us.[23-25]

The Holy Spirit, also called the "Spirit of truth,"[26] is the great Counselor who was sent by God to testify about the truth of Jesus

---

If you hold to my teaching, you are really my disciples.
Then you will know the truth, and the truth will set you free.
(John 8:31-32) [20]

He appeared so that he might take away our sins.
(1 John 3:5)[21]

That if you confess with your mouth, "Jesus is Lord,"
and believe in your heart that God raised him from the dead,
you will be saved.
(Romans 10:9)[22]

Repent and be baptized, every one of you, in the name of
Jesus Christ for the forgiveness of your sins. And you
will receive the gift of the Holy Spirit.
(Acts 2:38)[23]

And you also were included in Christ when you heard the
word of truth, the gospel of your salvation. Having believed,
you were marked in him with a seal, the promised Holy Spirit.
(Ephesians 1:13)[24]

And this is how we know that he lives in us:
We know it by the Spirit he gave us.
(1 John 3:24)[25]

And I will ask the Father, and he will give you another
Counselor to be with you forever—the Spirit of truth.
(John 14:16-17)[26]

And it is the Spirit who testifies,
because the Spirit is the truth.
(1 John 5:6)[27]

Christ,[27,28] and to guide us further into the truth as we live out our lives on this earth.[29,30]

There are always consequences for rejecting the truth and following lies.[31,32] Once we receive the truth, God wants us to "hold on to it,"[33] and not be swayed by people who try to distort the truth.[34] We must stand firm in the truth,[35] and not exchange the truths of the Bible for the lies of the world.[36]

When the Counselor comes, whom I will send to you from the Father, the Spirit of truth who goes out from the Father, he will testify about me.
(John 15:26)[28]

All this I have spoken while still with you. But the Counselor, the Holy Spirit, whom the Father will send in my name, will teach you all things and will remind you of everything I have said to you.
(John 14:25-26) [29]

But when he, the Spirit of truth, comes, he will guide you into all truth.
(John 16:13)[30]

But for those who are self-seeking and who reject the truth and follow evil, there will be wrath and anger.
(Romans 2:8)[31]

They perish because they refused to love the truth and so be saved.
(2 Thessalonians 2:10)[32]

They must keep hold of the deep truths of the faith with a clear conscience.
(1 Timothy 3:9)[33]

Even from your own number men will arise and distort the truth in order to draw away disciples after them.
(Acts 20:30)[34]

Stand firm then, with the belt of truth buckled around your waist.
(Ephesians 6:14)[35]

Once we know the truth of the Bible, we cannot fool God by pretending to follow the truth and then deliberately keep on sinning. If we try to do this, we are in danger of being judged by God and going to hell.[37]

In the final analysis, our journey as Christians is a journey towards truth. In a similar manner, our journey into mental health follows this same path.

Believing in the truth has a profound influence on our thought life. Once we become Christians, God expects us to bring our thinking into line with the truth (See, Lesson 29: Thinking, Healthy).

> They exchanged the truth of God for a lie, and worshiped and served created things rather than the Creator—who is forever praised. Amen.
> **(Romans 1:25)**[36]

> If we deliberately keep on sinning after we have received the knowledge of the truth, no sacrifice for sins is left, but only a fearful expectation of judgment and of raging fire that will consume the enemies of God.
> **(Hebrews 10:26-27)**[37]

Lesson 32

Unemployment

"Commit to the LORD whatever you do,
and your plans will succeed."
(Proverbs 16:3)

Unemployed: without a job; out of work

It's not uncommon for people to find themselves out of work or in jobs that they don't want or like. If you are feeling lost or fearful, turn to God for help and guidance. Seek His will for your life and do not give up hope.

Synopsis

If you are a Christian, realize that God has a plan for your life. His plan is for you to prosper and to stay out of harm's way—to give you hope and a future.[1] Your current situation may appear disastrous and you may be feeling desperate. However, remember that your problems are not too big for the creator of the universe and no matter what has happened, all things (even unemployment) can be used by God for your benefit.[2]

If you currently have a job, even one that in your eyes is not very desirable, you should give thanks to God and consider remaining

---

"For I know the plans I have for you," declares the LORD,
"plans to prosper you and not to harm you,
plans to give you hope and a future."
(Jeremiah 29:11)[1]

And we know that in all things God works for the good of those
who love him, who have been called according to his purpose.
(Romans 8:28)[2]

in your current employment until God opens up another door.[3] It may be that God wants you to stay in your situation until He calls you to do something else.[4]

Whatever your job, work at it with all your heart, as if you were working for the Lord and not for man.[5] Remember that there are many different ways that you can serve God.[6,7] Try not to compare your job to that of others,[8] and take comfort in the fact that all hard work brings a profit.[9]

If you are currently unemployed, try not to become lazy.[10,11] Laziness typically leads to poverty.[12]

Brothers, each man, as responsible to God,
should remain in the situation God called him to.
(1 Corinthians 7:24)[3]

*As long as it is day, we must do the work of him who sent me.
Night is coming, when no one can work.*
(John 9:4)[4]

Whatever you do, work at it with all your heart, as working for
the Lord, not for men, since you know that you will receive an
inheritance from the Lord as a reward.
(Colossians 3:23-24)[5]

There are different kinds of service, but the same Lord.
(1 Corinthians 12:5)[6]

There are different kinds of working,
but the same God works all of them in all men.
(1 Corinthians 12:6)[7]

Each one should test his own actions. Then he can take pride
in himself, without comparing himself to somebody else,
for each one should carry his own load.
(Galatians 6:4-5)[8]

All hard work brings a profit,
but mere talk leads only to poverty.
(Proverbs 14:23)[9]

The fool folds his hands and ruins himself.
(Ecclesiastes 4:5)[10]

Finally, if you are out of work, try not to chase fantasies and "get rich quick" schemes.[13] Such schemes often lead to grief, ruin, and destruction.[14,15]

God's Guidance

Being out of work or not making enough money to support yourself and/or your family can be extremely anxiety provoking. However, God does not want us to live in fear.[16-19] Your Heavenly Father is

---

Lazy hands make a man poor,
but diligent hands bring wealth.
(Proverbs 10:4)[11]

A little sleep, a little slumber, a little folding of the hands
to rest—and poverty will come on you like a bandit
and scarcity like an armed man.
(Proverbs 6:10-11)[12]

He who works his land will have abundant food,
but he who chases fantasies lacks judgment.
(Proverbs 12:11)[13]

Some people, eager for money, have wandered from the faith
and pierced themselves with many griefs.
(1 Timothy 6:10)[14]

People who want to get rich fall into temptation and a trap
and into many foolish and harmful desires that plunge
men into ruin and destruction.
(1 Timothy 6:9)[15]

Do not let your hearts be troubled and do not be afraid.
(John 14:17)[16]

Don't be afraid, just believe.
(Mark 5:36)[17]

The Lord is my helper; I will not be afraid.
(Hebrews 13:6)[18]

God is our refuge and strength, an ever-present help in trouble.
(Psalm 46:1)[19]

Your Father knows what you need before you ask him.
(Matthew 6:8)[20]

completely aware of all your needs.[20,21] He encourages us to trust in Him[22] and turn to Him in prayer.[23-25] We are to present our requests to Him, and find the peace that comes with turning everything over to God.[26] Our Lord promises that He will never let the righteous fall,[27] and that He will provide for our basic needs of food and clothing.[21,28]

If you are unemployed, one of the best things you can do is totally submit *your* will, to *God's* will.[29] Stop trying to figure everything out using your own limited brain and reasoning abilities.

So do not worry, saying "What shall we eat?" or "What shall we drink?" or "What shall we wear?" For the pagans run after all these things, and your heavenly Father knows that you need them.
(Matthew 6:31-32)[21]

When I am afraid, I will trust in you.
(Psalm 56:3)[22]

Is any one of you in trouble? He should pray.
(James 5:13)[23]

The prayer of a righteous man is powerful and effective.
(James 5:16)[24]

If you believe, you will receive whatever you ask for in prayer.
(Matthew 21:22)[25]

Do not be anxious about anything, but in everything, by prayer and petition, with thanksgiving, present your requests to God. And the peace of God, which transcends all under-standing, will guard your hearts and your minds in Christ Jesus.
(Philippians 4:6-7)[26]

Cast your cares on the LORD and he will sustain you; he will never let the righteous fall.
(Psalm 55:22)[27]

Consider the lilies of the field, how they grow; they neither toil nor spin, yet I tell you, even Solomon in all his glory was not arrayed like one of these.
(Matthew 6:28-29)[28]

Submit yourselves, then, to God.
(James 4:7)[29]

The situation is probably much bigger and more complicated than your own limited capacity to make sense of things.[30-33] Just turn things over to God, let go of all fear and anxiety, and let God help you find your path and direction in life.[34]

In the final analysis, being unemployed may turn out to be the best thing that ever happened to you. In your weakness,[35,36] you may

---

His wisdom is profound, his power is vast.
(Job 9:4)[30]

Great is our Lord and mighty in power;
his understanding has no limit.
(Psalm 147:5)[31]

"For my thoughts are not your thoughts,
neither are your ways my ways," declares the Lord.
(Isaiah 55:8)[32]

Where is the wise man? Where is the scholar? Where is the philosopher of this age? Has not God made foolish
the wisdom of the world?
(1 Corinthians 1:20)[33]

Trust in the Lord with all you heart and lean not on your own understanding; in all you ways acknowledge him,
and he will make your paths straight.
(Proverbs 3:5-6)[34]

For when I am weak, then I am strong.
(2 Corinthians 12:10)[35]

The Lord upholds all those who fall
and lifts up all who are bowed down.
(Psalm 145:14)[36]

Look to the Lord and his strength;
seek his face always.
(Psalm 105:4)[37]

I can do everything through him who gives me strength.
(Philippians 4:13)[38]

choose to look to God and His strength,[37,38] and seek His will for your life.[39,40] In your hopelessness, you may turn to God and find hope.[41-43]

Finally, remember that God's plan for your life may not be the plan that you have always had in mind.[44-46] In fact, this may be the perfect time to turn back to God and seek His will for your life.[39] If you are doing what God has chosen for you to do, your plans will always succeed.[47]

Teach me to do your will, for you are my God;
may your good Spirit lead me on level ground.
(Psalm 143:10)[39]

Your will be done on earth as it is in heaven.
(Matthew 6:10)[40]

Anyone who is among the living has hope.
(Ecclesiastes 9:4)[41]

Sustain me according to your promise, and I will live;
do not let my hopes be dashed.
(Psalm 119:116)[42]

May the God of hope fill you with all joy and peace
as you trust in him, so that you may overflow with hope
by the power of the Holy Spirit.
(Romans 15:13)[43]

In his heart a man plans his course,
but the Lord determines his steps.
(Proverbs 16:9)[44]

Many are the plans in a man's heart,
but it is the Lord's purpose that prevails.
(Proverbs 19:21)[45]

There is no wisdom, no insight, no plan
that can succeed against the Lord.
(Proverbs 21:30)[46]

Commit to the Lord whatever you do,
and your plans will succeed.
(Proverbs 16:3)[47]

Lesson 33

Weak/Tired

"Never tire of doing what is right."
(2 Thessalonians 3:13)

Weak: lacking in strength; vitality
Tired: worn out; lacking in energy

We all feel weak and tired at times. But feeling weary and exhausted is not always a bad thing. God can use our weakness to let His light shine through us. If we turn to God when we are tired and "burnt out," He will give us comfort and strength, show His mighty power, and refresh our hearts and souls.

Synopsis

We do not have to be physically or emotionally strong in order to serve God; in fact, it is to God's great delight that He uses the weak to shame the strong.[1] When we acknowledge our weakness and dependence on God, He can begin to work powerfully within us. The apostle Paul went so far as to boast about his weakness,[2] and delight in his hardships and difficulties.[3] He recognized that

---

God chose the weak things of the world
to shame the strong.
(1 Corinthians 1:27)[1]

Therefore I will boast all the more gladly about my
weaknesses, so that Christ's power may rest on me.
(2 Corinthians 12:9)[2]

That is why, for Christ's sake, I delight in weaknesses,
in insults, in hardships, in persecutions, in difficulties.
(2 Corinthians 12:10)[3]

when he was weak, and let God work through him, it was then that he became truly strong.[4]

If you are working for the Lord and feeling exhausted, do not give up. Never tire of doing what is right,[5] or grow weary doing good.[6] Try to keep your zeal for life and your spiritual fervor.[7] Put your hope in God and He will renew your strength.[8] Turn to the Lord and let Him recharge and energize your batteries.[9]

God's Guidance

If you are feeling weak and overwhelmed by life, look to the Lord and His might.[10] God promises that He will give strength to the weary and increase the power of the weak[11] He will reach down

---

For when I am weak, then I am strong.
(2 Corinthians 12:10)[4]

Never tire of doing what is right.
(2 Thessalonians 3:13)[5]

Let us not grow weary in doing good, for at the proper time we will reap a harvest if we do not give up.
(Galatians 6:9)[6]

Never be lacking in zeal, but keep your spiritual fervor, serving the Lord.
(Romans 12:11)[7]

Even youths grow tired and weary, and young men stumble and fall; but those who hope in the LORD will renew their strength.
(Isaiah 40: 30-31)[8]

To this end I labor, struggling with all his energy, which so powerfully works in me.
(Colossians 1:29)[9]

Look to the LORD and his strength; seek his face always.
(Psalm 105:4)[10]

He gives strength to the weary and increases the power of the weak.
(Isaiah 40:29)[11]

from heaven and take hold of us;[12] He will sustain us and make us great.[13] Regardless of our own human limitations and frailties, we are able to do all things through God who strengthens us.[14]

If you are tired and worn out, turn to God for rest.[15] Scriptures tell us that God is the only true source of rest and peace for our souls.[16] He alone can refresh our hearts and give us renewed energy for life.[17]

He reached down from on high and took hold of me;
he drew me out of deep waters.
(Psalm 18:16)[12]

You give me your shield of victory, and your right hand sustains me; you stoop down to make me great.
(Psalm 18:35)[13]

I can do everything through him who gives me strength.
(Philippians 4:13)[14]

*Come to me all you who are weary and burdened,
and I will give you rest.*
(Matthew 11:28)[15]

My soul finds rest in God alone;
my salvation comes from him.
(Psalm 62:1)[16]

Refresh my heart in Christ.
(Philemon 1:20)[17]

TOPICAL INEX

A

Abortion, *9-14*
Addictions, *15-23*
Adolescent Guidance, See "Adolescent Rebellion"
Adolescent Rebellion, *24-30*
Adultery, 104, 105, 182, 184
Afraid, 39, 41, 42, 58, 67, 84, 87, 144, 220, 222, 231, 232
Alcoholism,
Anger, *31-38*, 71-72, 129
Anxiety, *39-42*
Argumentative, 107, See "Quarrelsome"
Ascension, 58

B

Backsliding, *43-52*
Bad Company, 26
Baptized, 56, 194, 226
Beastiality, 184
Belief, *53-61*, 146, 149, 162, 211, 214, 218, 224
Boastful, 128, 235
Born again, 21, 44, 56, 225

C

Cheerful, 80
Child Abuse, 184, 185
Child/Children, 9, 11, 24, 74, 140, 141, 142, 143, 144
Christ, Who He Is, *62-65*
Citizenship, *66-69*
Communication, *70-82*
Compassionate, 31, 37, 79, 82, 94, 127, 203, 222
Complacent, 45
Conceit, 128, 169, 170
Confess, 13, 21, 22, 60, 100, 102, 121, 156-158, 161, 193, 194, 217, 226
Considerate, 68, 81, 127, 128, 129, 134, 161
Corporal punishment, 142, 143, 145

Counselor (Holy Spirit), 22, 59, 107, 210, 226, 227
Cross-dressing, 184
Crucified/Crucifixion, 58, 166

D

Death/Dying, *83-90*, 114
Deception, 76, 188, 205, See "Lying"
Depression, *91-103*
Devil, 33, 36, 37, 46, 51, 52, 80, 158, 195, 204, 205, 206, 207, 209, 210, 211, 212, 214, 217, 224, 225
Disaster, 32, 167, 220, 221
Discipline, 24, 26, 27, 42, 48, 49, 118, 142, 143, 144, 145, 221
Dishonest, 77, See "Steal"
Disobedience, 43, 54, 66, 68, 84, 189, 197, 204
Divorce, *104-107*
Doubt, 160
Drug Addiction, 17
Dying, See "Death"

E

Encourage/Encouraging, 81, 153, 200
Envy, 16, 38, 127
Eternal Life, 14, 53, 61, 83, 85, 92, 96, 108, 123, 126, 179, 188, 191, 196, 223, 226
Evangelism, 157, See "Witness"
Evil, 13, 18, 19, 20, 27, 29, 32, 40, 45, 48, 50, 51, 52, 54, 56, 70, 72, 75, 76, 90, 101, 128, 129, 130, 146, 147, 148, 149, 151, 158, 160, 163, 165, 170, 184, 186, 188, 190, 191, 192, 195, 199, 200, 204, 205, 206, 207, 208, 209, 210, 211, 215, 216, 219, 227

TOPICAL INDEX

F

Faith, 22, 25, 39, 42, 43, 45, 47, 50, 51, 55, 70, 81, 85, 96, 100, 107, 112, 126, 146, 148, 150, 151, 152, 156, 160, 162, 170, 172, 186, 199, 203, 211, 217, 218, 221, 227, 231
Fear, 27, 39, 42, 66, 144, *See* "Anxiety"
Forgive, 23, 79, *108-111*, 129, 151, 158
Forgiveness, 9, 13, 23, 59, 101, 103, *108-111*, 158, 187, 193, 194, 196, 226
Fraud, 77
Fruitful, 181

G

Gambling Addiction, 19
Glorified Body, 86
Gluttony, 16
Good News, 56, 59, 87
Gossip, 70, 78
Greedy, 19, 183
Grief, *112-115*, 221, 231
Guidance, 1, 7, 24, 91, 102, 106, 107, 132, 140, 143, 156, 213, 214, 219, 229
Guilt, 33, 100, 102, 119, 158

H

Happy, 25, 80, 97
Hardship, 150, 219, 221
Healing, 35, 80, 141, 156, 197, 198, 199
Heaven, 13, 29, 53, 58, 59, 61, 64, 67, 82, 83, 84, 85, 86, 87, 88, 89, 90, 92, 96, 101, 110, 112, 114, 118, 125, 128, 133, 138, 146, 147, 151, 153, 155, 157, 158, 159, 161, 163, 165, 174, 189, 197, 200, 204, 212, 234, 237
Hell, 42, 53, 60, 61, 74, 85, 87, 187, 207, 228
Helpless, 24, 91, 94, 95

Holy Spirit, 11, 17, 18, 19, 22, 53, 55, 59, 60, 92, 98, 100, 102, 107, 159, 165, 177, 178, 185, 194, 195, 206, 210, 211, 214, 217, 224, 226, 227, 234
Homosexuality, 19, 183
Hope, 23, 35, 45, 46, 72, 84, 91-94, 113, 114, 131, 138, 142, 152, 192, 200, 202, 203, 211, 220, 229, 234, 236
Hopeless, 91, 92, 93, 94, 131

Humility, 22, 32, 68, 81, 128, 163, 167, 168, 169, 170

Husbands, 129, 134, 161
Hypocritical, 33, 47, 116, 117, 118

I

Incest, 184
Insult, 75, 146, 147, 149
Illness, 197, 199

J

Jealousy, 16
Joy, 12, 25, 29, 52, 92, 97, 98, 113, 114, 127, 145, 159, 164, 201, 212, 217, 234
Joyful, 80, 81, 98, 152, 153, 221
Judgmental, *116-120*

L

Laziness, 230
Lord's Prayer, 155-158
Love, 14, 38, 79, 100, *121-131*, 140, 141, 157, 203
Lukewarm, 45, 51
Lust, 18, 183, 184, 185
Lying, 70, 76-77, 79, 130, 188, 206

TOPICAL INDEX

M

Marriage, 39, 104, 105, 106, *132-135*, 181, 182
Miracles, 57, 94, 95, 131, 198
Mock, 16, 74, 75
Money, 19, 20, 33, 45, 46, 125, *136-139*, 160, 231
Murder, 12

O

Obedience, 24. 25, 26, 28, 29, 30, 32, 67, 69, 87, 123, 144, 163, 197, 218, 225 *See* also "Disobedience"
Obesity. *See* "Gluttony"

P

Pain, 55, 90, 112, 113, 143, 146, 197, 198, 199, 201, 202
Parenting, 24, *140-145*
Patient, 35-36, 38, 71-73, 79, 93, 126, 127, 141
Peace, 37
Pedophilia, 184
Persecution, *146-150*
Perspective, 36, 73, 74, 92, 98, 109, 136, 200, 221
Plans, 93, 229, 234
Pornography, 15, 24, 184
Poverty, 16, 20, 39, 140, 144, 219, 220, 230, 231
Prayer, *151-166*, 205, 213
Pride, 128, *167-170*
Prostitution, 19, 182, 183

Q

Quarrel/Quarrelsome, 35, 36, 72, 73, 78, 128

R

Rebuke, 33, 116, 119, 120
Rebellious/Rebellion, 24, 27, 30, 31, 197

Refuge, 91, 97, 130, 157, 220, 221, 222, 231
Repent, 9, 13, 30, 56, 79, 87, 101, 109, 111, 116, 118, 121, 187, 188, 193, 226
Riches, 92, 97, 136, 137, 156, 196
Righteous, 29, 31, 33, 34, 40, 66, 70, 72, 80, 81, 82, 95, 97, 99, 108, 145, 160, 163, 190, 191, 192, 196, 210, 211, 219, 225, 232

S

Sad, *See* "Depression"
Salvation, 21, 41, 49, 56, 61, 86, 92, 166, 185, 192, 197, 211, 226, 237
Satan, 45, 51, 54, 106, 182, 189, 197, 204, 205, 206, 207, 208
Scripture(s), 1, 4, 7, 9, 28, 29, 31, 39, 45, 52, 90, 92, 106, 107, 110, 118, 119, 132, 133, 135, 136, 138, 141, 171, 182, 184, 217, 218
Second Coming, 60, 86
Self-Esteem, Low, *171-180*
Servant, 12, 46, 67, 74, 96, 147, 169, 195
Sex, Normal, 17, 18, 24, 132, 181-184
Sexual Addiction, 15, 17, 18
Sexual Offenders, See "Sexual Sin"
Sexual Sin, 19, *181-187*
Sickness, 197, 198, 199
Sin, 159, *188-196*
Sinful Nature, 16, 17, 21, 22, 34, 54, 186, 189, 191, 194, 196, 204, 215
Slander, 34, 68, 75, 77, 78, 81, 127
Sorrow, 15, 43, 102, 113, 114, 201, 203
Spanking, 142, *See* "Corporal Punishment"

TOPICAL INDEX

Steal, 77, 188
Strength, 44, 50, 52, 93, 94, 95, 99, 122, 130, 135, 177, 202, 203, 211, 213, 222, 231, 233, 234, 235, 236, 237
Suffer, 18, 39, 53, 54, 113, 146, 147, 148, 149, 197, 200, 221
Suffering, 57, *197-203*
Swearing, 75-76
Sympathetic, 82, 127

T

Temptation, 21, 158, *204-213*
Thankful, 52, 134, 152, 221
Thinking, Healthy, 7, 22, 106, 212, *214-218*, 225, 228
Tired, 235
Trouble/Hardship, *219-222*
Troubles, 163, 219, 221, 222
Trust, 39, 40, 41, 92, 130, 200, 220, 232, 234
Truth, 20, 22, 26, 46, 49, 56, 59, 60, 61, 64, 66, 77, 79, 83, 85, 95, 98, 100, 107, 113, 118, 119, 129, 130, 162, 164, 176, 187, 189, 195, 205, 209, 210, 214, 215, 216, 217, 218, *223-228*
Truthful, 76, 79, 130

U

Unbelievers, 85, 133
Unborn Baby, 9, *See* "Abortion"
Unemployment, *229-234*

W

Weak/Tired, *235-237*
Weakness, 114, 165, 201, 233, 235
Will of God/God's Will, 22, 98, 123, 155, 163-166, 176, 185, 217, 200, 221, 232

Wisdom, 20, 24, 42, 54, 73, 79, 102, 127, 128, 135, 139, 143, 145, 156, 164, 168, 196, 209, 224, 225, 233, 234
Witness, 77
Wives, 104, 129, 134, 135, 161, 243,
Work, 4, 7, 10, 45, 51, 148, 195, 202, 204, 205, 206, 207, 216, 224, 229, 230, 231, 235, 236
Worry, 39, 144 *See* "Anxiety"
Worthless, 91, 95, 171